The Power
of Strategic
Thinking

Other Books by Michel Robert

The Power of Strategic Thinking

Lock in Markets, Lock out Competitors

Michel Robert

McGraw-Hill

New York   San Francisco   Washington, D.C.   Auckland   Bogotá
Caracas   Lisbon   London   Madrid   Mexico City   Milan
Montreal   New Delhi   San Juan   Singapore
Sydney   Tokyo   Toronto

McGraw-Hill
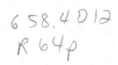
A Division of The McGraw·Hill Companies

ISBN 0-07-135777-7

All art is © copyright 1982 Decision Processes International. All rights reserved. Revised 1998.

The sponsoring editor for this book was Betsy Brown, the editing supervisor was Patricia V. Amoroso, and the production supervisor was Modestine Cameron. It was set in Palatino by North Market Street Graphics.

Printed and bound by Quebecor Arcata/Martinsburg.

To the four most important women in my life:

My wife, Ellie—who taught me the importance of sharing;

My daughters Emma and Samantha—who taught me the importance of giving; and

My late mother—who taught me the importance of reading and writing.

Contents

Preface

The premise of this book is that, for successful companies, competition is irrelevant. This is a concept that is totally contrary to that espoused by most strategy consultants today. Why do we have opposing views? The answer is a process called *strategic thinking*.

Decision Processes International (DPI) began developing the strategic thinking process in the mid-1970s. Our firm has been perfecting it ever since. The concepts you will be introduced to here are the result of our participation in over 400 sessions with *real* CEOs of *real* companies, discussing *real-time* "strategy" *online* with their management teams.

Unlike other concepts of strategy, developed by so-called gurus while sitting in business school libraries, our process was developed while sitting in the corporate "war rooms" of major and emerging corporations in dozens of countries and in a wide array of industries.

There are two methods used to develop concepts of management. One is based on so-called empirical evidence. This method is predominantly practiced by university professors who study organizations from the outside and try to re-create the reasons that certain companies succeed while other fail. They then publish a book detailing their "findings," without ever speaking to anyone from those companies or validating their "findings" in the real world. It is only *after* their book has been published that they get invited into the companies they wrote about. It is then that the flaws of their concepts are uncovered and another fad passes us by.

The other approach is called the experiential method. It consists of sitting alongside and observing chief executives of major organizations in an attempt to identify the concepts of management they practice, usually by *osmosis*. This is the school I belong to. Over the last 25 years my partners and I have worked with hundreds of companies as "insiders" and have been able to extract the concepts of strategic thinking from their heads. We then transformed these individual concepts into a codified process, which we handed back to these same executives. Only after we had validated the concepts by applying them to real businesses, and getting extremely good results, did we start writing books.

My first book appeared in 1981, after several years of validation, and the present text is my eighth book on the subject. All the interviews in this book are with *real* CEOs of *real* companies who have used our process over long periods of time. To them, the process of strategic thinking is not a fad. Rather, they view it as a necessary instrument of management and use it to manage the business on an ongoing basis.

Unlike many other approaches, our process has *stood the test of time*. For example, Glen Barton is the third Caterpillar CEO that our firm has had the privilege of working with over the last 14 years. Our relationship with Mike Harnetty and 3M dates back to 1980—20 years. Kurt Wiedenhaupt of API was our first client, also in 1980.

A similar relationship holds with the other CEOs who have graciously offered to talk of their experience with our process. I wish to thank them all for their confidence in our company and their patronage over the years.

Good reading!

Mike Robert

The Power of Strategic Thinking

1

Do You Suffer from Competitor Obsession?

Are you obsessed with your competitors? Are your competitors the first thing you think about when you get up each morning and the last thing on your mind when you go to bed at night? Are competitive tactics and techniques constantly surprising you?

If so, you have a *me-too* strategy and it's not working. Time for a rethink. A me-too strategy will never put your company in a position to dominate its competitors and, possibly, even to make competition irrelevant.

A me-too strategy is *imitation* strategy and, although *imitation may be the finest form of flattery, it is the worst form of strategy*. No company gains at the expense of a competitor by imitating that competitor's strategy.

The reason is simple. The competitor has set the rules of play and understands those rules much better than the imitator does. The competitor has in place an organization to police and enforce those rules. And the competitor probably has more resources than the imitator does. It's a little bit like playing blackjack or roulette against the house. No matter how much money you bring to the table, you eventually will lose! Why? The odds range from 1:1 to 1:0 in favor of the house. You eventually will lose!

Winning Requires a Distinctive Strategy

At Decision Processes International (DPI) we have worked with more than 400 companies across a wide spectrum of industries and countries over the last 20 years. Throughout that time, we have observed that winning companies never pursue a strategy of imitation. Winning companies have a strategy that is *distinctive,* one that sets them apart from their competitors. Their view of competition is to look over their shoulder periodically to make sure that the gap between them is getting wider and wider. This is true in just about every industry.

Does Intel have any competitors that it worries about day in and day out? Not really! Advanced Micro Devices (AMD) has a heck of a competitor in Intel, but Intel does not spend anywhere close to the amount of time worrying about AMD that AMD spends worrying about Intel.

Does Wal-Mart have any competitors? Not really! JCPenney, K-Mart, and Sears have a heck of a competitor in Wal-Mart, but Wal-Mart does not spend anywhere close to the amount of time worrying about them that they do about Wal-Mart.

Does Microsoft have any real competitors? Not really! Oracle, Sun Microsystems, and a host of other software companies have a heck of a competitor in Microsoft, but Microsoft does not spend anywhere close to the amount of time worrying about them that they do worrying about Microsoft. In fact, Microsoft was taken to court, not because it did anything illegal, but rather because it *outthunk* its competitors and literally locked them out of certain markets.

In the investment banking industry, Goldman Sachs is recognized by all parties—clients *and* competitors—as being the best in the industry, and that by a wide margin. The people at Goldman Sachs know it. Even new recruits are quickly indoctrinated in the notion of how superior Goldman is and how inferior its competitors are by comparison. Somewhat arrogant, but the Goldman concept of viewing competitors has worked extremely well—thank you!

The word "strategy" has a military origin. It comes from the Greek word for "office of the general." Over time, it has taken on a number of connotations, such as "the task of planning and deploying large-scale, combat operations." Or "the use of stratagems in business, games, courtships, or war." My favorite, however, is the view of strategy as "a maneuver designed to trick, or surprise, the enemy." A proactive, offensive strategy that keeps surprising competitors and makes these competitors irrelevant is the *ultimate strategy.* On the other hand, a me-too strategy has severe negative consequences.

Imitation Can Be Suicidal

It can even be said that an imitation strategy is not conducive to corporate health. In fact, it may be suicidal. That is, it can lead to the demise of a corporation. Examples abound.

For many years, a UK company called International Computers Limited (ICL) offered computers that were IBM copycats. That strategy worked only in protected markets that favored British companies. However, when these markets were deregulated, customers wanted the real thing—and that was an IBM mainframe. So long ICL! After many years of struggle and retrenchment, the company reinvented itself, and today it is strictly an integrator of other companies' computers and only a fraction of its former self in size.

Chrysler thought it had hit on a winning strategy back in the late 1970s and early 1980s, when it came up the concept of positioning itself as the "American Mercedes." Its cars were modeled after Mercedes cars, down to comparing its logo with Mercedes' and pointing out the similarity. That strategy led to Chapter 11. Car buyers wanted the real thing even though Chrysler offered them me-too cars for half the price!

Another car manufacturer struggled along for years while pursuing a strategy of imitation. In this case, however, it was imitating one of its own. And that is the Mercury Division of the Ford Motor Company. For over 60 years, Mercury was a replicate of some other Ford model. As a result, Mercury's market share was stuck at 3.3 percent for more than a decade, and the division hemorrhaged red ink for several years. It was only in 1998, under a new division president, that a *distinctive* strategy was formulated to design and market cars that would set Mercury apart from its competitors. The first redesign was the Cougar, a sports car that bears no resemblance to its predecessor. And the strategy is working. In six months, the division sold over 22,000 cars, most of them to first-time Mercury customers. The division now has a long list of new models under development, all of which will seek to distinguish themselves from their competitors. Look for the red ink to turn to black soon!

In yet another part of the automobile industry, a company called Autonation is struggling. Its strategy is a direct knockoff of that of rival Carmax. The reason is the same: imitation breeds disaster.

In a different industry, that of office supplies, a distant third is OfficeMax, far behind Office Depot and the leader—Staples. The reason, again, is the same. OfficeMax is a clone of Staples. In fact, it borrows a bit from Staples and a bit from Office Depot, a two-pronged imitation strategy that will lead to disaster twice as quickly!

In the television broadcasting industry, Rupert Murdoch's Fox Network and Ted Turner's CNN are soaring while the three original networks—ABC, CBS, and NBC—are all struggling. All three are following the identical strategy, and all three play musical chairs each year to see which network will capture 22 percent and which one will have 21 percent or 20 percent of a market that is diminishing each year. CNN and Fox have a *distinctive* strategy and are growing.

Another company that is on a suicidal path (but probably doesn't know it) is Lowe's, which is attempting to imitate Home Depot's strategy—down to having its employees wear red aprons versus the orange ones at Home Depot. Although Lowe's is doing well now, it is only because there are enough markets to enter to allow two competitors to thrive. The test will come when the markets are saturated with "big box" stores and a dogfight ensues. I'll place my bet on Home Depot!

A Distinctive Strategy Controls the Sandbox

The ideal competitive position to be in, naturally, is to have *no* competition. The ultimate strategy, in other words, is one that makes competitors *irrelevant*. In order to achieve this ultimate strategy, a winning company needs to formulate and deploy a strategy that is distinct enough from its competitors to allow the company to *control and/or influence the terms of play* in the sandbox it has chosen, lock in its target markets, and lock out undesired competitors.

The contrary is also true. If your strategy does not allow you to control, or at least influence, the terms of play, that is a clear indication that your strategy is not working. Wrong strategy—time for a rethink.

Craig McCaw, of Cellular One fame, entered the cable television business before switching to the cellular phone arena. Why the switch? As he explained to *Forbes* magazine, "We were never going to have a major influence on the cable business. Cellular was a place where we thought we could make a difference." McCaw was obviously looking for a sandbox where he could control or influence the terms of play. And did he ever.

Control or Influence: A Definition

Let's explore what we mean by control of the terms of play. Which company has been in total control of the computer sandbox worldwide for over 50 years? The answer: IBM. Has ICL controlled the terms of play? Has DEC? Has Unisys? Has Wang? Has Honeywell-Bull? The answer is no. IBM has been in total and complete control.

Which companies have been trying to "influence" the terms of play in the hardware side of the computer sandbox? That is, which ones are not yet in total control but have influenced the terms of play to their benefit? The answer: Dell, Compaq, Sun, Hewlett-Packard, and, for a short time, Apple. The other 150 competitors are not even in the sandbox, because their strategy is neither controlling nor influencing the rules of play.

From the 1920s until the early 1970s, General Motors was in total control of the automobile sandbox. But then came the Japanese and the German manufacturers. Today GM has half the market share it used to have and no longer controls, or even influences, the rules of play. In control along with Toyota and Honda is Daimler, which recently indicated its influence by purchasing Chrysler. Ford has attempted to influence the rules by introducing some models that allow it to distinguish itself from the pack, and has been able to maintain its market share.

There was a time, not so long ago, that whatever American Airlines did, all other airlines did sometime after. In those days, American controlled the skies. Then along came Southwest. And American no longer is in control of the industry. Nor is Delta, Northwest, or TWA.

The aircraft manufacturing industry used to be controlled by Boeing, with McDonnell Douglas a distant second and Lockheed a faraway third. Then along came Airbus with its "fly by wire" strategy and whoops, even mighty Boeing has had its share of hiccups. Another recent entrant into this sandbox is the Canadian company Bombardier, which is trying to influence the rules by pursuing a strategy that promotes the midsize jet (20 to 60 passengers). This strategy has caught both Boeing and Airbus off guard and has been very successful.

Hertz used to dominate the car rental industry, with Avis trying harder but never able to catch up. Today, while these two are chasing each other with identical strategies, Enterprise enters the fray with a totally different strategy, and steals the number-one position without Hertz or Avis having even noticed.

Companies Unshackling Themselves from an Imitation Strategy

For years, National Semiconductor lived in Intel's shadow, making me-too chips that resulted in corporate performance that got worse and worse. Brian Halla, who replaced Gil Amelio as CEO in 1996, has come up with a new strategy in an attempt to differentiate the company from Intel. That distinctive strategy is to make chips for appliances other than PCs, which is Intel's domain. Halla is betting the farm that today's "dumb" appliances will become "smart" appliances, equipped with all sorts of information that enables the owner to operate them more effectively. If Halla is right, National could finally extricate itself from Intel's shadow.

Besides Toyota and Honda, there is one other Japanese car company that is doing better since it stopped imitating its competitors and converted to a distinctive strategy. Like Mazda and Nissan, Subaru for many years offered me-too models. In 1996 the company decided not to "fight head to head," as President George Muller explained at the time. The company bet its future on the all-wheel-drive concept and eliminated front-wheel-drive models from its product offering. The new strategy positioned Subaru cars as rugged on- or off-road vehicles that could compete with sport utility vehicles and small trucks. The strategy is working. Sales have climbed to more than $3 billion per year and the company has announced record profits.

Sandboxes Controlled or Influenced by Key Players

Table 1-1 lists companies that are either in control or influencing the rules of play together with companies that are not and, as a result, are struggling.

Table 1-1. Control Versus Influence

Industry	Total control	Influence	Neither
Automotive	Toyota Daimler	Honda Chrysler	Nissan Mazda
Computers	IBM	Fujitsu	Bull
Airlines	Southwest	American Delta	TWA Midway
Broadcast	CNN	Fox	ABC CBS
Machinery	Caterpillar	Komatsu JCB	FIAT/Hitachi
Car rental	Enterprise	Hertz/Avis	Budget
Aircraft	Boeing	Airbus Bombardier	BA Aerospace
Beverages	Coca-Cola	Pepsi	7-Up
Distribution	FedEx	UPS/DHL	Airborne
PCs	Intel	Apple	AMD
Retail	Wal-Mart	Sears	JCPenney K-Mart

The Key to Control
of the Sandbox

The key question to ask about companies that control the sandbox they have chosen to play in is: How have they achieved their position of dominance and locked out competitors to one degree or another? The answer: By changing the rules of play!

Caterpillar, Inc.

CATERPILLAR ®

▲

The Turnaround of the Century

Glen Barton
Chief Executive Officer

You see them wherever you go, anywhere on earth. Where there's a road going through, a dam going up, a cellar hole being dug, they're there— Caterpillar's big (and now even small) yellow construction machines.

For the last 75 years, Caterpillar has worked to establish its global dominance of the construction equipment industry. Today it is one of the most consistently successful companies in the world, despite recent challenges posed by the "Asian flu." The success is largely due to its distinctive product-driven strategy, anchored by a worldwide network of Cat dealers—a unique capability, unmatched and probably unmatchable by any of its competitors. With sales of over $20 billion, Caterpillar stock is the perennial leader in the heavy equipment category.

But things weren't always this good.

Facing the Global Challenge

Twenty years ago, after six decades of uninterrupted growth, Cat had a close brush with death. The company had been charging ahead, doing battle in the marketplace with its traditional American competitors—

International Harvester and several others. And, as usual, Caterpillar was winning. Then, without much warning, new offshore competitors entered the fray—most importantly, Komatsu, a Japanese maker of construction equipment. The entire market was caught by surprise.

As CEO Glen Barton, who was president of the Solar Turbines division at the time, describes it, "We had been under strong attack by Japanese companies, particularly Komatsu, and had lost a lot of money over a three-year span of time as we tried to come out of a global recession and defend the market positions we had against the Japanese at that time. Komatsu specifically had set out a global challenge to encircle Caterpillar, and overcome us in all market areas."

As then-CEO George Schaeffer put it, "For years Caterpillar was a rocket. We could do no wrong. Then our business underwent profound changes. We had 60 years, all very successful, in which we built what *we* said customers wanted and needed. Then suddenly, the whole ball game had changed."

Don Fites who was Cat's president then, and who retired as CEO in 1999, remembers, "By the late 1980s, we'd experienced a decade without any real shareholder value being created. We were concerned about our Japanese competitors. When I joined the company, all our competitors were American companies. And they were all put out of business by the Japanese and Europeans, who are fierce competitors. *Survival* was a word we talked about around here."

Caterpillar, for the first time in its six-decade history, was in serious trouble. Competitors such as Allis-Chalmers and International Harvester were sinking fast, with Caterpillar not far behind. It was indeed a grim period in Cat's history. Never having faced this particular type of challenge before, Caterpillar management struggled to come up with a plan to deal with it.

"The game Komatsu was playing was to come into these markets with very low prices," Barton recalls. "By pricing the equipment at 25 to 30 percent lower than ours, Komatsu was inviting people to try its equipment, to use it as an alternative. We had price competition from other U.S. manufacturers at the time, but their price differentials were typically 15 to 20 percent, not the 25 to 30 percent we were seeing from Komatsu. Also, the Komatsu product brought a better level of durability and reliability than the other competitive products. And because of the weak yen, Komatsu could do this and still be profitable."

But Cat wasn't going down without a fight. It took every action it could to stave off the losses, buying time until it could come up with a turnaround strategy.

"A lot of people had written us off as they had many Rust Belt American companies," Barton remembers. "We went through a period of time in which we closed a lot of factories and tried to become a low-cost source, not necessarily to compete on price, but to make a profit on the prices at which we were already selling our products. We wanted to concentrate on *selling value*; we still do that today. We believed, and still do, that our products have more value than competitors' offerings. With the combination of performance, reliability, resale value of the product, and the ultimate life of the product, I think we retain that distinct advantage today. But in order to compete we had to sell our products at a price where we couldn't make any margin, and obviously we couldn't do that forever."

As Komatsu systematically went after Caterpillar's business outside the United States, Cat managed to hold its ground. It wasn't until the company began to feel the pressure on home turf that Cat was forced to find a new approach to running its business or follow its U.S. competitors into oblivion.

"Komatsu had been making inroads outside the United States, not much inside the United States," says Barton. "When it started taking us on in the home market, we bit the bullet and decided that we had to maintain our market position regardless of circumstances, until we could get our own house in order, which we then embarked upon doing."

An Abundance of Advice

Cat's management went about the task of seeking the best advice it could find among America's top business minds. As Barton recalls, "We went through a number of different consultants who worked with us. Among several others we had the top strategy consultant at the time, Michael Porter, and Noel Tichy, a facilitator who had worked with General Electric on its breakout process. At the same time, we were in the process of visiting other corporations to see what they had done and what guidance they could provide us."

Said former CEO George Schaeffer, "We were floundering despite help from the top consultants available. We had too much good advice."

By some turn of luck, Cat executives came across DPI's strategic thinking process, which was then a new methodology for strategy creation, one that would leverage *their* knowledge, not that of a consultant.

"We were looking for help on how to develop strategy and create a new organizational structure. Somewhere or other we came across Michel Robert's name and the DPI process and invited him down to make a presentation to our group. We were all impressed by the simplicity of his approach. Rather than spending two or three years getting the background material that a traditional strategy consultant like Michael Porter might have wanted before he was ready to move forward, the DPI process offered us a much more straightforward approach. It was one we'd feel comfortable working with and get faster results, which at that time was important," Barton states.

"I will always remember a comment Mike Robert made to us at a meeting early on, that 90 percent of what we needed to know to restructure our business was already in the heads of the people in that room. And, I think, if we contrasted that with Porter's approach, he would have said that less than 5 percent of what we needed to know was in the heads of our people in the company. The real number is probably somewhere in between, but Mike's point hit home with us." This basic concept of the DPI process struck a resonant chord with Caterpillar executives, many of whom had been with the company for 30 years or more. They believed, and continue to believe today, that no consultant could acquire the knowledge base or credibility necessary to tell a unique company like Caterpillar how to run its business.

The group also knew that because of the dire nature of its situation, action was needed immediately and getting involved in protracted consulting studies would only bog Caterpillar down.

"The idea of going out and doing a lot of surveys of individual market segments and collecting a lot of information about customer groupings and logical fits of customer groupings didn't appeal to us at all. We'd already done some of that and it didn't work all that well," says Barton. "Some of these projects never end; they just keep rolling along and become bigger and bigger, and longer and longer, and more involved. I think we all welcomed and still appreciate the fact that there's a finite course that you go through with DPI. In the last ten years, we have used it many times and when we undertake the strategic thinking process we know that there's an end. When we get to the end, there are decisions we're going to make and directions we're going to take and move on from that."

Hard Truths Emerge

During the first sessions on strategic thinking, some hard truths began to emerge. As Schaeffer said at the time, "Mike and his process helped us sort everything out. We knew that we were moving in a more orderly and focused fashion. We saw it all—businesses entered without commensurate expertise, misunderstood market shares, and so on. It was priceless. Noses got bent out of shape, but when noses get bent out of shape you generally get better decisions."

Says Barton, "The thing that impressed us as we moved through DPI's process with Mike Robert was the fact that, first off, he became an excellent facilitator for us. With all the people who had worked with us before, we would come up against a touchy issue and we'd get stuck. I think that one of the things we learned was that the DPI process is very good for facilitating the meetings and keeping us talking even though we would come up against a roadblock from time to time. These were sometimes very sensitive issues to a lot of people, and the directions that the group might decide to go were maybe disappointing to certain individuals within the group. But Mike drove the process, drove us through considerations of what kind of company we wanted to be, whether we were a product- or market-driven company, or a technology- or manufacturing-driven company. We logically arrived, through the process, at what we thought we were and what we still think we are today, which is a product-driven company. That helped us a lot as we moved forward in trying to strategize how we could better organize this product-driven company to serve the needs of the marketplace."

One of the most pressing issues the group recognized was the need for a complete reorganization of its structure into smaller units dedicated to specific product categories. This, the executives reasoned, would strengthen their product-driven strategy by bringing decision making closer to the market, and thus make Cat far more nimble and responsive. The company was restructured from what was a functionally driven organization into profit-center divisions, originally 14, growing to more than 20 today. Said Don Fites, "We completely redistributed accountability broadly, holding profit centers accountable for their own plans."

Two new units were created immediately, but full reorganization took a firm shove from an influential board member, who, seeing the wisdom of the conclusions reached in the DPI process, pushed them to compress their time frame for a complete reorganization.

Barton remembers how it happened. "We were creating the divisions. After a lot of debate we got eight or nine people to pretty well agree on what we thought the different divisions of the company should be; we got the executive office at that time to buy into that. Lou Gerstner was on our board. At that point he was still with American Express. We had created the first two divisions and Lou asked the question at a board meeting, 'When do you intend to go forward with the reorganization of the rest of the company?' And, frankly, within the company at that point in time, within the executive offices, there was a three/three split in terms of whether we should go forward with the whole reorganization of the company at once or whether we ought to wait until we had some experience with the first two divisions before we proceeded with the balance. So Lou spoke up again, as only Lou can do, and said, 'Look guys, my biggest concern is that you're going to reorganize this company over a two- to three-year period of time and find yourselves organized differently, but operating in the same manner that you're operating today.' He added, 'The only thing I can say to you is that if you're going to cause people to change the way they do things, you've got to follow through on this plan you've made and reorganize the whole company at the same time.' We moved forward and we never looked back.

"I think the reorganization is the most significant thing that has happened as a direct result of the DPI process and I think we had a total turnaround in our company in recent years as a result of it," Barton states.

As the divisions were created, they too went through the DPI process to establish their own strategy and agree on a list of critical issues. The Big Cat geared up and went on not only to survive, but to stage one of the most dramatic and sustained turnarounds in history. The company had successfully fended off its death threat, and almost immediately began to reestablish its dominant position.

Throughout the 1990s, Caterpillar posted impressive gains in sales, profits, and market share, in spite of recessions and a protracted labor dispute. In 1997, of all the stocks tracked by *The Wall Street Journal*, Cat stock was cited as third overall in five-year shareholder return. The company's sales have grown from about $8 billion in 1989 to over $20 billion today, and it has a market presence in virtually every nation. At the verge of the next century, Cat is one of the world's most solid performers by nearly any measure. Komatsu and the surviving competition are still there, but they no longer represent an apparent threat to Cat's survival.

As Don Fites said in 1997, "As far as the shareholders are concerned, it's the creation of shareholder value that has been rather spectacular." He also credited the DPI process with being the major catalyst that made this remarkable turnaround possible.

Opening a New Market by Changing the Rules

More than a decade after its initial recognition of a product-driven strategy, Caterpillar continues to refine the concept, and its product mix. One new line of products—and more importantly, the way it is being marketed—is opening a lucrative opportunity in which Caterpillar has never before been a player. The new line increases sales in such a way as to allow Caterpillar to use its vast dealer network as a strategic advantage once again.

As Barton explains, "The entrance that we're making today into the compact construction equipment business for the rental market is driven in large part by us changing the rules of the game. Rental of small construction equipment is an industry that has been growing very rapidly in recent years. Most of that growth is occurring through the consolidation of independent rental dealerships into larger companies that want the purchasing leverage to buy their equipment manufacturer-direct. If we would participate under their rules, we would have to bypass our dealer organization, which we refuse to do. So we've changed the rules of the game a bit and decided to get our dealers into the rental services business."

The opportunity is so significant that Caterpillar has designed and built a line of small construction machines specifically for the rental market.

"A key part of the plan was having the right equipment for the rental services business," Barton says. "And that's how the investment we've been making in our compact construction equipment line pays off. This type of equipment is the staple of the rental services fleets. It's much smaller than the equipment that we would typically produce. They rent it on a different basis; the small machines are what people like you and I would use if we decide on a Saturday to go and dig up our backyard. The new products we're introducing now are designed specifically for that type of use."

The program is being rolled out in North America and in selected markets outside the United States.

"We'll have some 300 stores in place by the end of 1999 in North America. We've got a number of stores in Latin America as well, and probably a couple hundred more will be up and running in Europe by the end of 1999," Barton reports. "We're creating a competitor for this new rental services opportunity and we're doing it with a marketplace that we already have access to because our dealers will buy our equipment. So we've used the strategic advantage of our dealer network to change the rules in our favor."

Building a Strategy
for the Next Century

Caterpillar management has revisited its corporate strategy periodically over the past ten years. Like many companies that have used DPI's strategic thinking process, Cat views it as a dynamic process that allows the company to change with the times.

Says CEO Barton about the upcoming strategy sessions, "I think it's time for us to look at our strategy again. We have a new chairman and we've also had this reorganization in place for almost nine years. It's time for us to go back and revisit our original vision, our mission, and our critical issues, and reexamine where we're trying to take the business, the kind of business we think we want to be, where the growth is within our businesses, and how we can better plan for the next decade. I think we will probably pick up the debate at a higher level than what we did the last time around and go back and reevaluate our strengths and weaknesses, which have changed some during that period of time, as well as evaluate some of the opportunities or threats.

"As we look at the world today, it's changing much more rapidly than it's ever changed before, with the influence of new information technology and so on. And the way we do business today versus how we may be doing business 20 years from now, it's hard to imagine that it's going to be the same. That has some tremendous implications for companies such as ours. As a result, I think it just says you have to continue to do this over and over and over. Once you've gone through the strategic thinking process and put your strategic plan in place, don't wait too long before you get another group started looking at it yet again to see if there's yet another need to do something differently because the world is really changing fast."

2
Changing the Rules of Play

How did Toyota, from a zero base, become one of the world's biggest car manufacturers? How did Craig McCaw, in just five years, build a company that he then sold to AT&T for $13 billion? How did Michael Dell manage to take the PC market away from Compaq and IBM? How did Home Depot come to dominate the building materials industry? How did Charles Schwab take the individual investor away from Fidelity? How did an obscure retail entrepreneur bring the giants of the retail industry—Sears, JCPenney, and K-Mart—to their knees? How did Ted Turner, of CNN fame, steal the market away from CBS, NBC, and ABC? How did Southwest become a giant of the airline industry at the expense of the so-called majors—American, Delta, and United Airlines? All these companies, and others to be mentioned shortly, have prevailed, not by *imitating* their competitors' strategy, but rather by *crafting a strategy that changed the rules of play.*

Companies That Changed the Game

Toyota emerged as the world's second-largest car manufacturer, not by imitating its competitors, but by changing the rules of the game to its favor. The story was best told by the Massachusetts Institute of Technology in the 1990 book *The Machine That Changed the World.* After World War II, Mr. Toyoda, Toyota's founder, came to America to see how the American giants, Ford and General Motors, manufactured and assembled cars. What he found was the famed *mass production system* that Henry Ford had developed at the beginning of the century. That system was designed to produce, on a vertically integrated basis and on one assembly line, the same model of car over and over again. The intent was to partition off the assembly into quick, repetitive tasks and lower the costs, thus making cars affordable to the "masses." The system depended on very large volumes in order to be cost-effective. The most successful example was the Model T, exemplified by Henry Ford's famous quote: "You can have any car in any color you want as long as it's black."

Mr. Toyoda's assessment was that the Japanese market could not generate the kind of volume that the U.S. market could and, therefore, that a mass production system was not suitable. He then set out to reinvent the production system. The result: a manufacturing process that became known as the Toyota production system and that has been emulated by Japanese companies almost as much as the Ford mass production concept was copied by American companies. Unlike Ford's system, the Toyota one assembles several different models on the same production line without having to make time-consuming, expensive changeovers. Mr. Toyoda found a way to *change the rules of play,* and this system has been at the root of Toyota's 40-year winning battle plan.

Craig McCaw's plan was also to grow a successful company by *changing the rules of play.* After he chose an industry "where he could influence the terms of play"—namely, the telecommunications industry—he set about to do just that. Instead of using copper wires, the long-standing norm in an industry dominated by AT&T, he chose to utilize a new technology called "cellular"—which, ironically, had been developed by AT&T. While AT&T went about defending its copper wire network, McCaw built a nationwide *wireless* network that almost brought mighty AT&T to its knees. In a last-resort attempt to stop the bleeding, AT&T finally bought out McCaw's company, Cellular One, for $13 billion. However, once the upstart was purchased, AT&T didn't know what to do with it. In the meantime, McCaw has set about changing the rules on his larger, supposedly more savvy telephone rivals one more time. While AT&T and the Baby Bells are warring each other, McCaw is in the process of building a network of low-orbiting satellites connected to wireless handsets offered by Nextel. The new system will have the capability of providing one-stop telephone communication anywhere in the world. AT&T may end up having to buy out McCaw a second time.

Michael Dell is another individual who, in a few short years, has built a computer powerhouse by *changing the rules of play.* Instead of marketing computers through retail stores, as the traditional rules demanded, the brash Texan decided to marry direct marketing techniques with the concept of on-demand, made-to-order computers. The result: a multibillion-dollar company that has the highest revenues per employee, the lowest inventory per employee, the highest return on capital, and a stock price that is climbing by leaps and bounds.

In 1997, Dell decided to change the rules again by extending its direct marketing method to the Internet. Months after it began selling directly to customers around the world, the company was booking over $10 million of orders *per day*. Today 80 percent of those orders are from new customers, many coming from recession-hit Asia, a market that has been abandoned by all the other computer vendors. In fact, Dell's success is causing all the existing makers of computers to rethink their approach to marketing their own products. The company that changed the rules may soon see its new rules become the industry standard. The turnabout demonstrates that a competitor can be so successful in changing the rules that an entire industry may feel threatened enough to convert to the new way of playing the game.

Two CEOs have already been concerned enough about the effect of Dell's strategy on their business to do something about it. Larry Bossidy of AlliedSignal has had Dell speak at conferences attended by all senior executives to sensitize them to this new way of conducting business and to think about how they can utilize the Internet to change the rules of play. If companies don't do this on their own, Bossidy warns, "somebody's going to come along and do a Dell Computer on you and destroy your business."

Similarly Lewis Platt, former CEO of Hewlett-Packard, stated that "Dell is forcing us to reorganize our whole sales end." A few weeks after making this statement, Platt announced that HP would be split into two separate public companies in order to "make each more nimble and responsive to customers."

Bucking the Retail Trends

Back in the late 1960s, Sam Walton decided to change the rules of the retail industry. In the little town of Bentonville, Arkansas, he opened his first department store, promising "low prices every day." The store was such a quick success that he soon opened nine more stores within a radius of 50 miles. To replenish his ten stores on a daily basis, he then placed a warehouse right in the middle. To ensure that his new distribution system was more efficient than any other retailer's was, he invested heavily in information technology, which was then in its infancy. Walton then cloned this distribution system in small towns all over the country and caught the Big Three—Sears, K-Mart, and JCPenney—asleep at the switch! While the majors kept imitating each other's strategy, Wal-Mart changed the rules of play, and spurted right past all three. Today, Wal-Mart has over 3000 stores generating over $160 billion in revenues, which makes Wal-Mart three times larger than its nearest competition—and the gap is widening each day.

In another branch of retailing, that of convenience stores, Chester Cadieux is about to become the Sam Walton of the industry. As CEO of convenience store and gas station chain Quik Trip, which operates primarily in the lower midwestern states, Cadieux is going up against the big boys—Mobil, Texaco, and 7-Eleven—and winning. How? By changing the rules of play. Instead of imitating his competitors, whose stores are stacked so high with all kinds of goods that they look cramped and ill-kept, Cadieux keeps his Quik Trip stores bright, airy, and tidy. They stock only high-volume, fast-moving goods and, even more notable, at convenience-type prices usually well below those of competitors. The result: the chain has 330 stores, and counting, which generate an average of $2 million of annual merchandise revenues and 3 million gallons of gas per store—compared with its competitors' $900,000 and 720,000 gallons respectively. Cadieux has now decided to invade Texas—7-Eleven's turf. If history repeats itself, 7-Eleven may be back in bankruptcy court again.

A few years ago, Anita Roddick changed the rules of play in the cosmetics industry by launching her Body Shop chain of stores rather than selling through department stores, which was the conventional way to go to market in that industry. Also, she offered only in-house products based on natural ingredients packaged in natural, recyclable material. Today, there are over 300 Body Shop stores all over the world.

Another European, Myron Ullman, is in the midst of changing the rules again. He has built a chain of 175 stores under the name Sephora by not doing what the department stores do. Unlike the department stores, which display products by brand in kiosks supplied by the manufacturer and staffed by a manufacturer's salesperson who "pushes" the product, Sephora stores display products by category. There is a lipstick section that displays all the brand names together. Then, there is a facial cream section, a mascara section, and so forth. Furthermore, there are no manufacturer's sales reps pushing the product. Instead, customers are encouraged to sample products at their own leisurely pace without being pressured. Ullman's strategy has the department stores in its crosshairs and has them scared to death. While their businesses are growing at the rate of 7 to 10 percent annually, Sephora grew at the rate of 55 percent last year and plans are to double the number of stores in the next 3 years. Ullman recently opened a flagship store in Rockefeller Center in New York City, right next to Saks. The jury is still out, but it will be an interesting battle to watch.

Changing the Rules More Than Once

In the financial services industry, one individual—Charles Schwab—has demonstrated an uncanny ability to change the rules of play not once, but several times. And each time he has tilted the playing field to his company's advantage and has made his competitors almost irrelevant. Schwab first changed the rules when he entered the business in the 1970s. His strategy was centered on the financial needs of the *individual investor.* Instead of having salespeople work on a commission basis, he hired people on salary. His staff worked three shifts per day and was available to its clients around the clock. He then set out to change the most cherished rule of this blue-blood industry by setting transaction rates that were half the industry norm. Furthermore, unlike his competitors, Schwab offered no research, one of the most costly services a broker extends. The company was profitable from day one.

In 1995 Schwab changed the rules to his advantage again when he introduced the One Source program, which permits investors to purchase a mix of mutual funds directly from Schwab rather than do so from each mutual fund company individually. The One Source program allows the investor to choose from a portfolio of over 700 funds without paying any commission whatsoever and to switch from one fund to another without any penalty. This concept completely revolutionized the marketing of mutual funds and caught the industry leader, Fidelity, totally off guard.

In 1997 Schwab went for a hat trick and changed the rules one more time. He introduced a program that allows investors to trade stocks online. In just 3 years, from a zero base, the company is now trading more than $4 billion per week—which is more than half the firm's total volume, and three times the volume of the next three competitors combined. Over 2 million of its 5.5 million customers, which represents a third of the firm's customer assets, are online.

And because online costs are lower than those of traditional trading, Schwab has started providing free research. Watch out Merrill Lynch. The future may not as bullish as your stampeding bulls suggest. More will be said about Merrill Lynch's current and future trauma in a later chapter.

Wayne Huizenga holds the distinction of successfully changing the rules twice, in two different industries, and he is now attempting to do it in a third. He made his first billion by changing the rules of play in the waste business. Historically, the waste business had been a highly fragmented industry with thousands of mom-and-pop operators serving small portions of individual municipalities. Huizenga was one of the first "consolidators," and his company, Waste Management, bought out thousands of these small operators and became the industry leader within a few years.

After leaving that business, Huizenga repeated the formula in the video rental business. This time, he built a chain of retail stores, called Blockbuster, from the ground up. However, the recipe was the same. He promoted a single brand identity, standardized operations that lowered costs, and opened over 1500 large stores that all displayed their product in the same manner. He made his second billion. And now Huizenga is trying for a hat trick in the used-car industry, where he is building a national chain by buying out hundreds of dealers around the country. His third billion is on the way.

New Entrants, New Strategies

If you were a golfer in the early 1980s, you would remember that the market for golf equipment was primarily the domain of two companies—Spaulding and Wilson. That is, until Eli Callaway hit the golf links and completely changed the rules of play by introducing the Big Bertha metal driver. The club face was almost twice the size of a traditional driver and resulted in more distance for the user. A number of other entrepreneurs took his lead and introduced everything from clubs made of special metals to putters of all shapes and sizes. Today, one can fill a golf bag with each club purchased from a different manufacturer. There has been an avalanche of new entrants into the market. Firms such as Adams, Cobra, Ping, Orlimar—to name but a few. And where are Wilson and Spaulding? In oblivion.

Ted Turner entered the broadcast business back in the mid-1980s and looked at the three major players—ABC, CBS, and NBC—none of which had had a significant shift in market share in 30 years. All three practiced the identical strategy and, as a result, all three played musical chairs each year to determine which one would have slightly better than a 20 percent share. Turner decided not to play the game that way and changed the rules. Instead of standard broadcast, he chose cable and satellite; instead of a variety-programming format, he adopted an all-news format; instead of staying domestic, he went international. Who made more money in the last 10 to 12 years? Ted Turner—by several billion!

In the highly competitive and price-sensitive trucking industry, one company is bucking the trend with a distinctive strategy that changed the rules to its favor. Most trucking companies in the United States have organized themselves to serve the just-in-time (JIT) inventory needs of their customers. As result, they have short-haul or long-haul routes and prefer back-to-back loads. Roberts Express of Akron, Ohio, does the exact opposite. Its strategy is to exploit breakdowns in the JIT system. Consider a car assembly plant in Detroit that receives its engines from another plant in Cleveland. When there is a breakdown in this system and the engine does not get there on time, Roberts Express steps into the picture. The company has 2000 trucks stationed around the country, on standby, waiting for such a call. While on the phone with the person from the car assembly plant, Roberts, using its proprietary satellite communication system, will locate the truck that is closest to the supplier's site and promise the customer to pick up and deliver the engine within a 15-minute window at both ends. Not only does Roberts get paid a premium for this service—in an industry where the lowest price is the name of the game—but its growth rate is substantially higher than that of any other company in the industry. Management at Roberts Express prays each night that companies continue to make the JIT time frames tighter and tighter.

The airline industry was, for a long time, controlled by American, Delta, and United. That was until Southwest Airlines arrived on the scene and completely changed the rules of play. Whereas the major airlines play a hub-and-spoke strategy, Southwest plays a point-to-point strategy; whereas the majors use multiple aircraft, Southwest uses a single aircraft; and whereas the majors have invested billions of dollars in sophisticated reservation systems, Southwest doesn't even have one! And which player is about to become the largest airline company in the world? You got it!

The airlines are about to suffer another shock, maybe even an earthquake. In mid-1998 an individual named Jay Walker started a company called Priceline.com, and the airline industry will never be the same. On its first day of operation, Priceline radically changed the rules of play. If you've had any amount of travel with the major airlines, you know that the same itinerary given to five ticket agents from the same airline will elicit five different prices, all exorbitantly high. Walker, using the Internet, has reversed that process and is putting the customer in charge of pricing and not the airline.

Priceline asks the customer what he or she is prepared to pay to get from A to B and then scans, over the Internet, the airlines' computers and asks for bids from the airlines. Since airlines are capacity-driven, the price is always matched but it is the customer that controls the price decision. The concept has caught on. In the first quarter of 1999, the company booked over 195,000 tickets—twice what it booked since it started up. The stock has done very well as well—thank you very much! It went from $16 to $130. And Walker has even found a way to lock out competition for at least 17 years—he has patented the entire system so that no one else can do what he does. In other words, a "virtual" monopoly.

In yet another industry, that of building materials, two individuals— Bernie Marcus and Arthur Blank—set out some years ago to change the rules of play. The building materials industry is a highly fragmented one with thousands of small, local "yards." Blank and Marcus came up with what has become known as the "big box" concept. Unlike the local yards, they built stores with over 100,000 square feet of merchandising space, and they stocked these with every imaginable home improvement product they could squeeze into that space. They then hired craftspeople—carpenters, electricians, and plumbers—as service attendants, provided these professionals with bright orange aprons, and encouraged them to stroll through the aisles looking for opportunities to assist customers. The result: over 1000 Home Depot stores generating well in excess of $30 billion in annual revenues. And the plan is to open two of these monster stores every week for the next few years!

The fast-food industry has been saturated with too many brands, too many stores, and too little profits for years. Most companies that own chains or franchises, such as PepsiCo, have been selling off these assets. Not many takers. There is one buyer, however. His name is William P. Foley II, CEO of CKE Restaurants Inc. His company is making profits by changing the rules. Instead of buying up healthy chains, CKE is a collector of badly managed chains. The company owns over 5000 restaurants under such brands as Checkers, Rally's, Long John Silver's, and Hardee's. Whereas CKE's competitors concentrate on building new stores in suburban areas, Foley concentrates on refurbishing old stores located in metropolitan areas.

These stores were usually the first ones built. Most are in prime locations with ample pedestrian traffic—traffic that didn't enter because the stores had been allowed to run down. Once spruced up, Mr. Foley has discovered, these stores reattract patrons and the profits roll in again.

Companies in the Midst of Changing the Rules

A company that is in the midst of radically changing the rules of play in an industry that has not witnessed much change in a long time is Amazon.com. The revolution it is bringing to book retailing is giving fits to Borders and Barnes & Noble. By selling books over the Internet, Amazon.com has found a way to tilt the playing field to its advantage while putting its two major competitors in very awkward positions. The numbers speak for themselves. While Barnes & Noble offers 200,000 titles in some of its stores, Amazon offers over 3 million, or 15 times more! While Barnes & Noble has several hundred million dollars tied up in bricks and mortar, Amazon has only one central warehouse. Whereas Barnes & Noble's stores cater to potential customers who live or work around each store, Amazon can sell to anyone, anywhere in the world, *anytime*. Barnes & Noble's sales per employee are $125,000; Amazon's are $675,000. Barnes & Noble has 27,000 employees with all the accompanying overhead costs; Amazon has 1600. Barnes & Noble turns its inventory over three times per year; Amazon does so 24 times. To purchase a book at Barnes & Noble, one must go in person; with Amazon, one simply clicks a key from one's home. The result: Amazon is growing at a rate of 306 percent compared with Barnes & Noble's 10 percent and is on its way to becoming a $10 billion company. It has even caused Barnes & Noble to rethink its strategy and forced it to build its own Internet selling method. Now Barnes & Noble is playing according to the rules set by Amazon and has two strategies at work simultaneously. This is bound to fail. Not only will Barnes & Noble not beat Amazon in its sandbox; it will probably start losing in its traditional sandbox.

Borders, facing the same threat from Amazon.com, has come up with a more ingenious response. Instead of imitating Amazon, Borders announced that it will print books on demand, in its stores, in 15 minutes. This is an attempt by Borders executives to change the rules back to their favor, and I suspect they will have more success than Barnes & Noble. Stay tuned.

Tilting the Playing Field

Two other companies that are attempting to change the rules as part of a strategy to tilt the playing field to their advantage are America Online (AOL) and a new entrant called PressPoint.

Why did AOL purchase Netscape? At the time that the acquisition was announced, many analysts wondered what the strategic motive was. CEO Steve Case's motive soon became evident. His intent was to neutralize Microsoft's strategy by changing the rules of play. Together with Sun Microsystems, the trio will be the only player with the capability to serve customers "end to end," as COO Robert Pittman explained at the time. In other words, the AOL/Netscape/Sun troika will be the only one with the software, hardware, and Internet access to enable companies to conduct their entire business—from the initial sales entry to the production schedules to the distribution center to the invoicing to the accounts receivable and payable—in cyberspace! Competition may do more harm to Microsoft than the Justice Department.

PressPoint is attempting to change the rules in one of the oldest industries around—newspaper publishing. For years, newspapers all over the world have seen the advent of electronics as a potential death threat and have made feeble attempts to offer electronic billboards to their subscribers as a defensive maneuver. PressPoint is going to do something very different that may appeal to a large number of frequent travelers. Instead of offering them news from around the world, it will offer people traveling abroad access to news from home—electronically. By signing up, a subscriber will be able to receive *local news* anywhere in the world. Lance Primis, the firm's CEO, may be the first electronic press lord.

The AT&T Saga

Yet another company that is finally trying to change the rules to its favor is AT&T, the former Ma Bell. Prior to its breakup by the Justice Department in the 1980s, AT&T had a monopoly and was in total control of the "sandbox." After the breakup, AT&T lost control of the sandbox and meandered from one flawed strategy to another while playing to rules set by MCI and the Baby Bells. Until Mike Armstrong came aboard in 1998. Within months, Armstrong crafted a strategy whose intent is to regain control of the sandbox by dramatically changing the rules against AT&T's competitors. While its competitors have different rates for calling on certain days, at certain times, and by various types of transmission, AT&T announced a flat rate of 10 cents per minute—using any transmission network, whether that be copper wire, cellular, or cable, for either local or long distance calls anywhere in the world, and at any time of the day or night. For the first time in a decade, AT&T has its competitors scrambling for a response and has them in a reactive mode instead of the other way around. The jury is still out on the soundness of this new strategy, but the company announced record earnings in the next two quarters following this change in direction.

AT&T has also decided to change the rules of play in a more fundamental way than just offering lower prices. Telephone signals are generally carried over copper wires. Once any competitor obtains control of that distribution system, the name of the game becomes one in which the low-cost provider wins. In the local markets, these wires are controlled by the Regional Bell Operating Companies (RBOCs), or Baby Bells. The system places AT&T at the mercy of its key competitors and thus, in a losing position.

Starting in the year 2000, AT&T CEO Mike Armstrong has decided to deploy a new system called Angel. Instead of wires, the company will install a small box on the side of your building that will connect to the phones inside and then transmit the signal from the building to its ultimate destination not through wires, but through the air to a series of antennae, which will then tap into AT&T's worldwide network. With this system, AT&T will be able to bypass the RBOCs' network, offer both local and long distance service on its own network, and unshackle itself from the RBOCs' stranglehold. If successful, Angel might lead to AT&T's revival and renewed dominance of telephony.

Mike Armstrong's attempt to change the rules to AT&T's favor intensified in late 1998 and early 1999 with the acquisition of cable companies TCI and MediaOne. In two quick strokes, AT&T became a formidable force in the cable business. AT&T has gone from being a company with a me-too strategy to one with a distinctive strategy that can offer over 60 million homes a complete bundle of services including local telephone, long distance telephone, cable television, and Internet access. In 18 short months, Mike Armstrong has transformed AT&T from the laggard in the industry to a potential powerhouse. Stay tuned.

Why Changing the Rules Works

One of the lessons we at DPI have learned is that significant shifts in market share do not occur by imitating a competitor's strategy. Rather, *significant shifts in market share occur only by going at the very essence of a competitor's strategy and changing the rules of play.*

In 1980 Xerox had 97 percent of the worldwide copier market. In 1985 it had 12 percent. Why? Canon came into the game and radically changed the rules of play. Instead of coming in with large machines, Canon came in with small machines. Instead of selling through a direct sales force, it went with distributors. Instead of leasing the machine, Canon sold it outright. It took Xerox five years to decide to sell through distributors, and it took the company seven years to wean itself from its leasing dependency—85 market-share points later!

When you change the rules of play on your competitors, you place them in a very awkward position. To deploy their own strategy, your competitors have put into place a certain organizational structure, certain processes and systems, certain skills and competencies, and certain compensation plans to conduct business in a certain manner. When you change the rules of play, you force your competitors to make very agonizing changes in the manner in which they conduct their business. And often they cannot bring themselves to make those changes. In other words, your competitors are *paralyzed* because you have neutralized their strategy. They are no longer on the playing field but are standing on the sidelines *not playing the game.* And while they are on the sidelines, you can make significant gains at their expense!

By now you are probably asking yourself: "How does a company go about formulating and deploying a strategy that will change the rules of play to its favor and grow at its competitors' expense, or lock them out completely?"

The answer to this vital question is for the company to have a clear and distinctive strategy that it is totally committed to and that leaves no room for ambiguity.

Roberts Express

roberts
express
A Caliber System Company

Discovering a New Driving Force on the Road to New Markets

Bruce Simpson
Chief Executive Officer

It's 9:30 Monday morning. The phone rings in the office of Jim, the plant manager. It's Alice, the lead person on engine assembly line 4. The news isn't good. Seems somebody forgot to schedule a crucial shipment of camshafts. They're on a loading dock 300 miles away at the company's other plant, and if they're not here by 4:00 P.M., the third shift is dead in the water.

Jim doesn't hesitate. "Have Alan call Roberts Express," he says. "They've bailed us out before." A few minutes later in Akron, Ohio, a Roberts customer assistance team (CAT) member, one of a couple of hundred on that shift, is on the case. Using the company's high-tech system of computers and integrated two-way satellite communications, he's located a truck in the vicinity of the pickup that's the right size for the load. The driver's accepted the load and the fire is all but out.

Situations like these have made Roberts Express one of the most successful trucking companies in America. Early recognition of an unfilled need enabled Roberts to craft a *distinctive* strategy, creating an opportunity outside the established rules of the trucking business. Started in 1947 as a

27

local Ohio trucking firm, Roberts really began to take off in 1980 when it hit on a market need no one else saw—delivering emergency shipments for the auto industry as just-in-time (JIT) inventory came into being. The company has since gone national, even international, and serves industries of every kind from automobiles to aerospace to pharmaceuticals.

Explains Bruce Simpson, Roberts's CEO, "We pioneered the market for what is essentially nonstop, door-to-door delivery—anytime, anywhere— and we guarantee it. We move freight of any size or weight. A large percentage of our shipments are for same-day or early-next-day delivery. As supply chain trends tighten inventories and manufacturers turn to just-in-time and other time-sensitive production methods, the need for our unique services has grown."

Deregulation Changes the Playing Field

The opportunity was created by the deregulation of the trucking industry. As electric utilities and the financial services industry have discovered, deregulation changes the playing field in fundamental ways, creating problems for established players and opportunities for those who are alert to them.

As Joel Childs, Roberts's vice president of marketing says, "When the regulatory environment changes, that's when the biggest opportunities arise." In Roberts's case, as deregulation changed the restrictions on existing routing structures, Roberts was able to create its unique service—one that had no competitors because such a service had not been allowed under the old rules.

As Childs explains, "In the old days under regulation, it was set up so that the least competitive entrant could survive. In trucking, there were two kinds of carriers. There were irregular routes that were truckload. And there were regular routes that were LTL—in other words, hub-and-spoke operations that handled freight en route. Roberts Express could not have gotten authority under the old structure because we are actually neither. We're much more of a needs-based situation. Needs are not taken into consideration in a regulatory environment. And what happens is that the provision structure becomes inappropriate and inefficient because it's not driven by customer need. It's driven by the historical regulatory structure. The other thing that happens is that when the regulations change, the sandbox becomes open.

"Companies in a deregulating environment should be looking for their models in transportation deregulation. Because there is one thing that all economic regulation has in common—inadequate, inefficient provision structures. Because the structures are not market-driven, they're regulation-driven, and they are invariably inappropriate. They were created to protect the present entrants and actually resist new ones. And it's especially true if you look at what's happening now in electric utilities distribution, for example. The rules are all going to change. They can't do it the old way."

Roberts didn't do it the old way. The company noticed a need in the market, matched it up with the new rules of play, and grew the business rapidly.

As Simpson describes it, "Today we have about 1800 trucks in five different sizes, stationed throughout North America. When our sophisticated call center in Akron, Ohio, receives a customer request for a shipment, our customer assistance teams (CATs) usually have a truck at the customer's pickup location in less than 90 minutes. And it's the right truck—matched to the size and weight of the shipment. The freight is then carried on a exclusive-use basis directly to the delivery destination. When we say we'll be on time, we mean it—within 15 minutes for pickup *and* delivery."

It sounds simple the way Bruce Simpson describes it, but considering the number of trucks, variety of sizes and types of shipments, unpredictability of customer needs, and vagaries of weather and traffic, the challenges are daunting. Add to that the fact that Roberts doesn't own the trucks (the drivers are all independent contractors) and the logistics seem insurmountable.

What makes it all possible is a high-tech system with integrated two-way satellite communications that Roberts has delivered over time. The system allows dispatchers to instantly locate and communicate with Roberts's trucks across North America. Specialized software selects the right truck, considering a wide range of factors that make the specific truck the best choice for both Roberts and the customer. Then, after the pickup, Roberts's system tracks the position of the truck within a few hundred yards so that progress can be reported to the customer if necessary. Any time there is a delay of more than 15 minutes, a Roberts CAT member is automatically alerted. This allows Roberts to act immediately to get the shipment back on track.

The network allows the company to offer "expedited trucking" on a coast-to-coast basis. For shipments requiring air transport, the company has a separate division called CharterAir®, and air charter services are also available in Europe through Roberts Europe. Building on this concept, Roberts has expanded its business base well beyond last-minute emergency shipments, finding new applications for its unique service.

"When we first started doing this," Simpson relates, "we would go to big companies and they would say, 'That's a unique, creative idea in logistics, to be able to respond that quickly with a truck dedicated to one shipment door to door, anywhere, faster and cheaper than air freight.' But then they'd say, 'We don't need that kind of service.' Then the phone would ring and there'd be an emergency. They'd suddenly need us and afterward they'd say, 'Great job, thank you. We made a mistake and you helped us fix it. We paid you a lot of money, but it was worth it. But don't tell anybody we used you. It's just this one time.' But then they would come back to us again and again."

These same customers gradually began to find new uses for Roberts's service—uses that were not based on fixing mistakes, but were built into distribution plans for special types of products in an evolution of the just-in-time chain from raw materials to manufacturing to distribution. "We began to get calls from those same companies saying that they were going to build us right into their value stream, to help them reduce inventories as part of their system," Simpson says.

Among the other extensions of the original service is the need to deliver time-sensitive products to market quickly, such as new computer chips, when they first become available.

Roberts has also looked for niches by changing the rules in more traditional trucking markets. In one case the company targeted the major van lines that offer special shipping for delicate products such as electronics, perfume, and food. Through its "White Glove Service," Roberts would offer the same special handling but on a dedicated same-day basis. Expecting a battle, instead the company was surprised to find a new relationship. One major van line realized that, through Roberts, it could offer same-day service to its own customers instead of turning them away when the timing of the shipment was impossible to meet within its own system. Roberts wound up with an office at the van line facility and a steady stream of new business!

Rolling Out a Future Strategy

There's no doubt that things were rolling along pretty well at Roberts. Even so, a couple of years ago, Bruce Simpson began to feel the need to look at the future shape of the company.

"We were growing dynamically. We were a successful company," Simpson says. "But I and others pondered every leader's challenge—to know your vision, your strategic priorities. I think we were doing everything absolutely well tactically, but we needed to fall back from the trees and look at the forest, to look out into the future."

It was then, in early 1997, that Simpson called in DPI to take his management team through the strategic thinking process. The approach appealed to Roberts because "it makes sense. It's pragmatic. And after you go through the assessment of your driving force and your business concept, you put into play a process that everyone understands and remembers. And out of that you have strategic goals and objectives that are shared and identified and monitored and you believe will work over time," says Simpson.

As the top management of Roberts Express went through the process, a surprising new road map for the future began to emerge. "We had the top 22 or 23 people at Roberts go through the process, and a very important part of that process was the debate over our future driving force. We really argued—and that's good. We like that kind of stuff around here. I like being surrounded by people who are smarter than I am, and our company's culture encourages people to speak up," Simpson states.

"We had been convinced that we were a service-driven organization. We had grown to be $150 million or $160 million by developing this service niche—same-day or early-next-day delivery—because of the needs of the marketplace. That's where we have positioned ourselves—faster and cheaper than air freight. And of course we'll continue to be in that business. But DPI's process took us through challenges that changed our thinking about how we'll grow in the future. We realized that our driving force isn't the service itself—it's the distribution system we have. So even though we provide this unique dedicated transportation service, the change in driving force implies that we can extend the business possibilities for a superior integrated communications network and a controlled delivery system that does things very effectively from a transportation, information, and customer satisfaction standpoint. Now we look at that distribution system differently and it opens up opportunities for new applications of our information system that we wouldn't have thought of otherwise."

The system, through its ability to locate and track objects anywhere on the map, is tremendously powerful and could be useful to a wide range of customers.

This shift in corporate mindset changes substantially where Roberts goes from here. "It opens up new possibilities for businesses we can get into, and it eradicates some of the businesses we had thought about getting into. Before, we might have been considering whether we should be expanding into different modes of transportation. Now we'd say, 'That's not a strength of our organization.' Now we have a clear reason to place a higher priority on certain components of the organization—like the information technology and electronic commerce. We wouldn't have thought of these things if we hadn't come to this realization about our driving force. Also, if we're going to consider acquisitions, we're going to make sure that we remember to determine whether the opportunity builds on that driving force. We're also beginning to use DPI's Strategic Product

Innovation® process to help us develop *new* products and services using strategic criteria that are consistent across all groups at Roberts.

The strategic thinking that now permeates Roberts Express affects a wide range of day-to-day decisions about resource management and planning. Major decisions, particularly, have a much stronger strategic component. Explains Simpson, "Now every time we do something from a technology standpoint, which is important around here, there is no disconnect between the CEO and the CIO. Every time we make an investment in technology, we ask ourselves questions based on DPI's concepts: How will this move help us change or influence the rules of play in our competitive sandbox? How can we leverage that driving force more effectively in terms of value to our customers and the information that we provide? The approach enables us to continue to differentiate ourselves and continue to add value. It allows us, as DPI says, to choose our competitors, manage our competitors' strategy, and neutralize their driving force, by changing the rules of play. Now when we make decisions about where we're going and why, we have a process in place. It's shared and understood by the leadership, and we speak the same language when we look to the future."

3

The CEO's Dilemma: Strategic Ambiguity

After more than 20 years of experience in the field of strategy, we at DPI have concluded that the key to business success *is not to outmuscle competitors operationally but to outthink them strategically.*

Strategy Versus Operations

Unfortunately, many executives do not understand the difference between strategy and operations. Understanding this subtle nuance is a key skill of a successful CEO. One simple way to illustrate the difference is to view strategy as *what* and operations as *how*. In other words, strategy is the kind of thinking that is "what we want to be" in nature, while operations is the kind of thinking that is "how to get there" in nature. Graphically, the difference is shown in Figure 3-1.

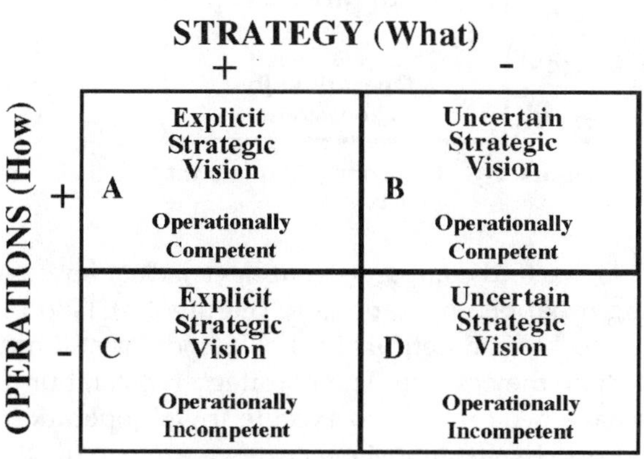

STRATEGY (What)

	+	−
OPERATIONS (How) +	**A** Explicit Strategic Vision — Operationally Competent	**B** Uncertain Strategic Vision — Operationally Competent
OPERATIONS (How) −	**C** Explicit Strategic Vision — Operationally Incompetent	**D** Uncertain Strategic Vision — Operationally Incompetent

Figure 3-1. The strategic thinking matrix.

In quadrant A, we find companies whose strategy is well articulated, well communicated, and well understood by everyone in the organization (Figure 3-2). These companies know what they want to become. Furthermore, they are very competent operationally. They know how to get there.

Figure 3-2. Companies in quadrant A of the matrix.

One such company is IBM under Lou Gerstner's recent formulation and deployment of a "cocentric computing" strategy. Other companies with clear strategies are Disney under Michael Eisner, Dell Computer under Michael Dell, Wal-Mart under Sam Walton and David Glass, and Home Depot under Bernie Marcus and Arthur Blank.

In quadrant B, we find companies that are operationally effective but strategically deficient (Figure 3-3). Many of the companies pursuing a me-too strategy fall into this quadrant.

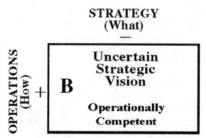

Figure 3-3. Companies in quadrant B of the matrix.

In quadrant C, we find companies that have a clear strategy; their difficulty is making it happen operationally (Figure 3-4). Good recent examples are the 130 to 140 competitors in the PC industry all trying to be the best "Wintel" clone they can be. Their strategy is clear, but unfortunately most of them have been unable to execute it well operationally, and the winners and losers change almost every day.

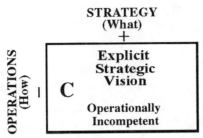

Figure 3-4. Companies in quadrant C of the matrix.

In quadrant D, we find the worst of both worlds (Figure 3-5). Unfortunately, the list of examples is not very long because if you find itself in this quadrant, you are not around long enough to talk about it.

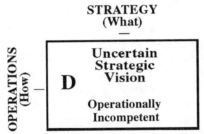

Figure 3-5. Companies in quadrant D of the matrix.

In which quadrant do you think most companies find themselves? I have asked this question of more than 3000 CEOs all over the world and the answer is always the same. Between 80 and 90 percent of these CEOs tell me that most companies reside in quadrant B: operationally competent but strategically deficient. Many CEOs even include their own company in this observation. In other words, most executives can keep the "numbers" coming out right quarter after quarter, but they don't have a shared understanding of what the company will look like as a result of all that churning. I call this the Christopher Columbus School of Management:

> When he left, he did not know where he was going;
> When he got there, he did not know where he was;
> When he got back, he couldn't tell where he had been!

Do you belong to this school? To find the answer to this question, you may want to go through the following assessment.

What Is the Strategic IQ of Your Organization?

The following survey will help you assess the strategic IQ of your organization in order to determine which quadrant you fall into. The survey is designed to be answered by the CEO and the management committee.

---

1. Do you have a well-articulated, clear statement of strategy?
   Yes—Score 10 ☐   No—Score 1 ☐

2. Could each member of your management team write a one- or two-sentence statement of that strategy without consulting the others?
   All could—   Some could—   None could—
   Score 10 ☐   Score 5 ☐   Score 1 ☐

3. Do you have your strategy in written form?
   Yes—Score 10 ☐   No—Score 5 ☐

4. Does your strategy statement serve as a guide in determining which future products, customers, and markets your company pursues?
   Frequently—   Sometimes—   Never—
   Score 10 ☐   Score 5 ☐   Score 1 ☐

5. Does your strategy statement serve as a guide in deciding which products, customers, and markets your company does not pursue?
   Frequently—   Sometimes—   Never—
   Score 10 ☐   Score 5 ☐   Score 1 ☐

6. Does your strategy statement serve as a tool in deciding how resources are allocated within your company?
   Frequently—   Sometimes—   Never—
   Score 10 ☐   Score 5 ☐   Score 1 ☐

7. Does your strategy statement serve as a tool in choosing which opportunities your company pursues and which ones it doesn't?
   Frequently—   Sometimes—   Never—
   Score 10 ☐   Score 5 ☐   Score 1 ☐

8. Have you ever sat down as a management team to try to obtain consensus as to the future direction of the organization?
   Regularly—   Once in a while—   Never—
   Score 10 ☐   Score 3 ☐   Score 1 ☐

9. Was consensus obtained, or are there still different visions of *what* the organization is trying to become?
   One vision—   Several visions—   No vision—
   Score 10 ☐   Score 1 ☐   Score 1 ☐

10. Do you have a *separate* process of strategic thinking to determine *what* you want to become as opposed to *how* you get there?
    Formal, codified process—Score 10 ☐   No process—Score 1 ☐

The respondents should answer the questions individually, without consulting one another, and their answers should be compared afterward.*

If all the members of your management team gave very similar replies, then you are in good shape. The wider the discrepancies in their replies, the less clear or understood your strategy is. You may want to entertain taking your management team through the process described in the remainder of this book.

Scoring Your Strategic IQ

For a numerical assessment of your strategic IQ, simply add up the scores next to each question you responded to.

Score: 100

You're perfect. There is no need for you to read the remainder of this book unless you don't know *why* you are so good.

Score: 70–99

There is some degree of ambiguity over strategy among the management team, with periodic disagreements over direction, particularly on significant issues. You are on the cusp of great success if this ambiguity can be removed. Your batting average is a few more wins than losses, but this average could be substantially improved by the removal of ambiguity. Exposure to a good strategic process would bring considerable value.

Score: 40–69

You are suffering from a severe case of "fuzzy" vision. The differing views of strategic direction among the management team results in erratic operational performance. There are numerous disagreements over strategic issues, and you are probably frequently surprised by competitive tactics. Failure to clear up this ambiguity will further erode operational results. It's time to bring a process into play to relieve the organization of this ambiguity and stop the bickering.

Score: 1–39

You are focused too tightly on operational issues and short-term results. Decisions are made on an event-by-event basis rather than within a set of

*You can obtain an objective assessment of these answers, along with an "audit" of your strategy, directly from DPI.

strategic parameters. There is continuous, and heated, debate among the management team over direction. As a result, decisions are frequently arbitrated and dictated by the CEO in order to break the stalemate. The company is in a me-too strategy mode and is frequently surprised by competitive tactics. Most actions are taken as a reaction to competitive initiatives. Time for a rethink.

Good Strategy, Bad Execution

"It's easy to develop a strategy; it's the implementation that's difficult." Over the years, we have heard this refrain from just about every CEO we have encountered. Our own experience shows, however, that the *formulation* of a strategy is as difficult as the implementation. We have also found several legitimate reasons why many CEOs have difficulty implementing a strategy when one is in fact in place.

The Strategy Is Implicit

Although most CEOs admit to being in quadrant B, it is a fact that many of them do have a strategy or, at least, the beginnings of a strategy. Unfortunately, the strategy is usually implicit, and not explicit, and resides in the head of the CEO. Most CEOs we know have great difficulty articulating their strategy to the people around them.

As a sector vice president of a Fortune 100 company once observed: "The reason I have difficulty implementing my CEO's strategy is because I don't know what it is!" To which we at DPI respond: "It's very difficult for people to implement a secret strategy."

Because CEOs have difficulty verbalizing their strategy, most of their subordinates are placed in the position of having to "guess" what the strategy is, and they may guess wrong as often as they guess right. It is by the decisions that are accepted or rejected by the CEO that they eventually figure out what the strategy is and what it permits and does not permit. This is called *strategy by groping,* and it usually takes people a long time to discover the line of demarcation between those activities that the strategy lends itself to and those that it does not. This time would be better employed by knowing the strategy from the beginning, since people may guess wrong as often as they guess right.

LESSON 1: People cannot execute a *secret* strategy.

The Strategy Is Developed
in Isolation

A second reason the CEO's strategy may not get the respect it deserves, and thus may not be implemented, is that the CEO has developed it unilaterally. Although the strategy may be brilliant, the management team was not involved in the *process* of formulating it and, therefore, has no ownership. As a result, people don't understand the rationale behind the strategy and will spend more time questioning it than deploying it. Meanwhile, the CEO becomes more and more impatient, unable to comprehend why people are not executing what the CEO views as a simple strategy.

Some CEOs may involve one or two executives in the formulation of a strategy. This is better than doing it alone but still not good enough to gain ownership. The *entire* management team must be involved in order to breed understanding and ownership.

LESSON 2: Strategy execution is not possible without ownership.

The Strategy Is Developed
Without Commitment

The "kiss of death" to any strategy—even a good one—is to impose it on the organization without commitment from the management team. Experience has shown that almost any strategy can be made to work, unless it is based on horrendous assumptions about the external environment. However, experience has also shown that almost no strategy will work if members of the management team are not committed to that strategy. They may, in fact, attempt to sabotage the strategy rather than implement it.

Many CEOs have used DPI's strategic thinking process even though they knew the outcome in advance. They did so in order to tap into the knowledge base of their people and to obtain commitment to the conclusions, so that implementation could proceed expeditiously.

LESSON 3: People do not execute a strategy unless they are committed to it.

Operational Managers Are Not
Good Strategic Thinkers

Most managers spend their entire careers in an "operational silo." In other words, they live in a function, or "slice" of the organization, and become accustomed to the day-to-day issues and the resolution of these effectively. With few exceptions, there are very few "strategists" in any organization. Most people are so engrossed in the operational, how-to activities that they do not acquire the skill of thinking strategically. Therefore, they have difficulty coping with strategic issues, especially if these are sprung on them out of the blue. Only when we rise above the silo and look at the business and its environment from 30,000 feet do we develop the skill to think strategically. It is only at that altitude that we start asking: "Why are we doing these things?" Many CEOs will, therefore, involve their management team in the process for the educational value alone.

LESSON 4: Operational prowess doesn't breed strategic ability.

The CEO's Dilemma

Once an organization decides that the time is ripe to invest management's time in an attempt to formulate a clear strategy for the enterprise, an important question arises: "Do we attempt to do this by ourselves or do we bring in a consultant to help us?"

This is the first dilemma a CEO must face. Our experience at DPI has shown that it is extremely difficult for any management team to get involved in an in-depth and highly qualitative discussion of the company's future direction *without outside help*. The reason is simple: these forums can deteriorate into highly subjective shouting matches with no productive outcome. Most CEOs, therefore, call in an outside consultant.

This brings the CEO to a second dilemma. There are two types of consulting that the CEO can call upon. The first is "content" consulting. Here the consulting firms "do it for you." They invade your organization with an army of 25-year-old MBAs, turn your drawers upside down for six months, and come back with a report that tells you what your strategy *should be!* Their rationale is simple: they consider themselves to be experts in the industry and more *knowledgeable* than you and your management team; therefore, their analysis and conclusions are going to be better than yours.

A major consulting firm attempted to buy our firm a few years back. One senior vice president of that firm said to me during the discussions: "Our stand is that we know more than the client about the industry and the industry's best practices. Therefore, we are in a better position to develop a strategy for the client than he can do for himself."

We at DPI have two big difficulties with this premise. First, we do not think that any outside consultant has the "right" to tell you what your strategy should be, since the consultant has no stake in your business.

When consultants leave, they leave you with the consequences. Second, even if two or three of our people were to live in an office next door to each of your key executives for a year, they would never understand your business as well as you and your key executives understand that business. Therefore, even if we came back with a strategy contained in a manual two feet thick, you and your people would pick it full of holes in five seconds flat, and the strategy would end up on a shelf very quickly. Early in my consulting career, when I walked into a room for the first time to work with the top 18 executives of Caterpillar, I met with a junior executive who had been with company 23 years and a senior one who had been there 42 years. What knowledge about their business could I bring to the discussions that did not already reside in the head of one or more of these executives?

A better approach, in our view, is for consultants to bring their clients a *process* that allows the clients to *do it for themselves.* This is known as "process" consulting. In other words, the consultant provides a structured process that allows management to formulate and deploy its own strategy. We bring the *questions* and we guide you through these questions in a systematic way, but it is *your input* going into the process and *your output* from the process. This approach breeds consensus, commitment, and, most importantly, ownership of the strategy by each member of the management team. It is as much *their* strategy as it is the CEO's. As a result, the strategy gets implemented more quickly and more successfully than one imposed on management by a third-party, outside consultant.

Using an outside "content" consultant to develop a strategy for you is akin to outsourcing your strategic thinking. Not only will you end up with a me-too, "off the shelf" strategy similar to that of your competitors; you will also fail to acquire the skill. In fact, you are now at the mercy of this third party forever.

As Kurt Wiedenhaupt, CEO of American Precision Industries, says of DPI's strategic thinking process: "I have been exposed to McKinsey, the Boston Consulting Group, and Bain, and I am sure they're intellectually sound, but they're not *of the people, by the people, through the people.* When it comes to executing the strategy, they are miles behind the DPI process. It's simply ownership." Amen!

We at DPI are convinced that as long as there is debate and ambiguity over direction, there is no effective execution going on. Therefore, a CEO must have a *process* that engages the entire management team in deciding the company's future direction. That process must be structured and objective in that it invites vigorous discussion during the work sessions but at the same time ensures commitment and ownership so that management can then concentrate on implementing the strategy rather than debating it. That process is called *strategic thinking.*

Bekaert, S.A.

⒀ BEKAERT

Shaping a Vision of the Future

Rafaël Decaluwé
Chief Executive Officer

When you got up this morning, took your clothes off a wire hanger, drove your car on steel radials across a suspension bridge, came home, rode your bike, and popped a champagne cork to celebrate your anniversary, you probably used Bekaert products at every turn. This Belgian manufacturer is a world leader in the steel wire and steel cord business.

With headquarters in Kortrijk, Belgium, the company has 60 plants in 20 countries, employing nearly 18,000 people worldwide. In 1995 Bekaert turned out about 1.8 million tons of wire, which sold for just under $3 billion. Its wire finds its way into a surprising array of products—including steel-belted radial tires, concrete reinforcing wire, steel rope for bridges, coat hangers, fencing, bicycle spokes, staples, and, yes, even 5000 tons of wire annually for champagne cork cages.

In steel wire, the company has basically three areas of business. The industrial wire business has a high-volume, commodity orientation and competes primarily with integrated steel companies. The specialty wire business makes custom wire products for individual customers. Another group produces wire fence—from cyclone fence to heavy-welded security fence.

The steel cord division holds a significant share of the steel-belted radial tire market worldwide. The typical car tire contains one or two pounds of this reinforcing material, a truck or bus tire as much as 20 to 45 pounds. In this part of the business, Bekaert's main competitors are also its customers—the major tire companies that also make steel cord.

"We are truly a global business," says CEO Rafaël Decaluwé (pronounced de-*cal*-oo-way). "It's a diverse business with various types of products that all come out of one raw material—wire that we source from the steel companies. We have businesses that are global, regional, or local and therefore have very different forms and shapes of management. I should add that because we have had a very long association with Japanese companies, we have a very strong TQM culture."

Decaluwé became CEO in October 1994, after serving as one of Bekaert's division managers. His first task was to define his role as CEO, and formulate an approach to the job.

"After interviewing and debating with a number of people, not the least of whom were the people on the board—who look at my rating sheet and my pay every year—I came to the conclusion that my primary task is shaping the vision of the company, communicating it, and getting it implemented. Now those are three things that are easily said, but not so easily done," he says.

His perception at the time was that the company was strong operationally, yet needed a vision to drive its performance in the future. He looked at the three basic approaches: existing "excellence" models proposed by Deming, Baldrige, and others; "solution-driven" consultants; and "methodology-driven" consultants. The first, he felt, were good tools for implementation, but didn't address vision. The second, he believed, would run the risk of not understanding the business, jumping to conclusions, and, most importantly, achieving low credibility with management. He settled on the third—in the form of the DPI strategic thinking process. "What I wanted was a methodology that involved the thinking of our own people. I would hope that the people who have been working in this business for 20 and more years would have a better view and understanding of what the business is capable of doing, and where it should go, than an outside consultant who comes in for three to six months, reviews and interviews in your organization, and then comes up with a so-called magic solution of what you should do for the next X number of years."

As the CEO looking at the organization, Decaluwé could see that "strategic thinking" was not a priority among his managers, and he had to sell the concept. "We made long-term plans that were mostly done by each business. They were number exercises without much *qualitative* thinking and analysis in my view.

"I felt that the numbers usually do not turn out anyway because they're fairly straightforward extrapolations based on existing assumptions. They really don't give you a lay of the land of where you are with your business versus competition versus the environment outside.

"What I was trying to get out of this process was really shortening the chain of thinking within the group. Then from a group perspective and within our different businesses, we would start from a fundamental analysis of the environment. We were looking to get a feel for strengths and weaknesses, and to have a much clearer, qualitative picture of the road ahead."

Decaluwé chose to use strategic thinking largely because of prior positive experiences with the process. "It goes back a little bit in history. I had used the DPI process when I was division general manager, to help the business climb out of the clouds. If I could compare it to an aircraft, it enabled us to make sure we had a clear sense of direction and continued momentum and drive in that direction, as we were entering blue sky," he states. "I was most happy with that process in my divisional responsibilities. I then took over as CEO of the group and felt that was one of the things we were lacking.

"To me, the first challenge was overcoming the skepticism of my own management that there was a need to go through a conceptual strategic exercise. These are mainly engineers and they deal with numbers. To do a qualitative assessment, to many of them, seemed unnecessary."

So the first challenge was to convince the management team of the need for a strategic assessment. "There was some question as to 'Why do we need to do this? Aren't we doing well anyway? What's the point of starting this sort of exercise?' So there I had to argue, preach, and reason with people to get them to believe that a strategic thinking exercise is important. After a while I was successful in convincing them to go through the process, when they came to understand that it does not present them with a solution, but *that they are part* of the solution. So once we got into the process, the skepticism went away because they felt that they all had a part to contribute in it. At the same time, once we had gone through the three-day session, what I call 'taking everybody through the funnel of the process,' not everything was smoothed over. But we had a chance to come back and refine what was said, and deepened the consensus and the commitment along with it."

Selecting a Driving Force

The nature of Bekaert's diverse businesses presented a challenge in the selection of a driving force. Some of its units sell industrial products that serve again as "raw materials," such as tire-reinforcing cord; others, such as the fence group, sell a finished product to consumers. Resolving the differences took some time.

"Several driving forces were tried out," Decaluwé remembers. "There were differences of opinion around the table. But then in the first three-day session, in subteams we each developed a possible driving force and then analyzed whether each was sensible as we looked at the various outcomes of pursuing that driving force. It led to a conclusion that two out of the three we were looking at were not the right answer. We were looking at capacity-driven, technology-driven, and product-driven.

"By process of elimination, clearly product could not be it, because we have a wide range of products. Mike Robert likes to say that when a product-driven company makes cars, its next product will be another car, and another car. That's certainly not the case for us. It's wire, but the applications are so diverse that you can hardly say that they're the same product in the end."

The group finally settled on technology as its uniting driving force. "We call it cold metal transformation and surface treatment, in the broad sense of the term," Decaluwé explains. "And for this technology we have over 10,000 applications."

The driving force then gave rise to areas of excellence and a set of critical issues. "Critical issues were the most important results. One key area was deepening and leveraging our technology across the businesses much better than we had done in the past. Another was focusing our international expansion much more in terms of geographic areas. At the same time, we came to understand that we needed to develop certain new competencies that we did not have up till now, and that would be important for success in the future. So, together with a never-ending cost reduction focus, at least it gave us some clear critical issues that have been driving quite a bit of the thinking and the actions that we have developed since that time."

Specifically, the management team identified five critical issues that would be essential to supporting the bridge between the present and future "pictures" of the company. They included developing greater depth in wire-drawing technology; leveraging that technology development; building capabilities in marketing, application development, and innovation (the areas of excellence associated with a technology-driven company); and developing a greater presence in Far East markets. And at the center of all those issues, enhancing the skills of the people and structure of the organization would become a priority.

In the steel cord division, three critical issues were identified: TQM with customers, cost reduction, and internal functioning. Each of these was broken down into several component parts—nine goals—as action items, and a triangle "logo" was created as a communication vehicle. This and other logos created to symbolize the company's vision and goals were to be used extensively as a means to keep attention focused on the new initiatives.

"Twenty people signed off on that. It's a tremendous bond between them," says Decaluwé. "And we would never change that unless those same people were back around the table. Today, I can walk into any plant in the steel cord division, point to that triangle logo, and ask any of the people working on the quality teams how what they're working on relates to the company's goals, and they will know."

From Concept to Implementation: Step by Step

Rafaël Decaluwé and his team have been careful to ensure that the strategy is not only articulated, but also continuously carried out and *refined*.

"Let's look at each of the steps. First, shaping the vision. I think of this as having three important pieces," says Decaluwé. "First of all, you have to understand where you are—what are we and where are we today? Also, you need to draw a picture of the future. That is your vision of what and where you want to be X number of years from now—you can say two years or five years or ten. And then I think the most critical part to it is, when you've painted the picture of where you want to be—how do we bridge the gap? We have actually created a bridge logo to symbolize that. On top of formulating the steps of how to get there, you also need a *clear sense of direction* of how you're going to move from where you are to where you're going.

"The next step—communicating the vision—has a lot to do with making sure that there is a clear sense of direction. You will, as a CEO, have to communicate it again and again—convincing, preaching, telling, arguing. That has been the most important challenge to me. You have to keep doing it—50, 100 times—and you have to do it each time with enthusiasm even though it may be becoming repetitive to you.

"The next step involves what I call deployment at lower levels—getting all the noses pointing in the same direction. Now deployment to me has to do with systematic translation of the general goals into concrete terms understandable to the level of the organization that you're addressing.

"If you go to one of your machine operators and you say, 'Your responsibility is processibility at the customer's plant,' if he's polite he'll say, 'Well what does that mean to me?' And if he's that polite to ask, then I think you ought to at least do one thing—bring the message to him in understandable terms. What I would say to him is, 'To you it's the diameter consistency and the coating consistency of that wire. And that's how you can measure your contribution to the goal.' It's very important that you don't leave people with lofty sorts of objectives that they cannot identify with or can do nothing about."

Bekaert's long-standing commitment to TQM is a very significant part of the execution of goals such as cost reduction and performance for customers. "We have the example of wire breaks—this is part of the cost reduction goal. Wire breaks in our process are very expensive because the weld in the product will give you more trouble in the next step and of course your machine uptime drops."

Just as the management team uses a rational process to formulate the strategy, teams at various levels use TQM tools, such as systematic problem solving, that are appropriate to their needs. Teams are then able to complete the tasks that make up the critical issues—in this case, reducing costs by identifying and eliminating specific causes of problems such as wire breaks.

"Putting a chart next to a machine where people can put another dot showing what they have accomplished is extremely powerful in terms of getting their commitment and ownership," Decaluwé believes.

"The progress that we've made on the critical issues is the result of assigning each one to a task force that will design answers to solve it, and a number of steps have already been taken. They're by no means finished, but at least I know that I'm now driving the business and making progress on the basis of those critical issues. And I can, at fairly regular intervals, gauge to what extent we are answering and continuously enhancing our response to those critical issues.

"It's taken hold. I wish we were further along in terms of implementing the critical issues, but a number of them have developed well. We have understood very clearly, for instance, why there were barriers built into leveraging technology across the businesses, and we have taken the necessary steps in order to get there much more rapidly than we would have otherwise done."

Keeping the Flame Alive

Once the critical issues begin to take hold, the CEO's role shifts to keeping the organization's attention and enthusiasm trained on those goals. And the CEO must continue to monitor and test and reevaluate. Bekaert's team has developed specific steps to ensure that this continues to happen.

"First of all, to ensure that the strategy is still correct, we've already done an update. So every other year we go to a short-form reassessment, and see if any of the key variables that are in the process have changed. We repeat the basic profile and, through communication, continue to update where we stand on the development and implementation of the critical issues. I do that twice per year in my communication with all the management employees in the group," Decaluwé explains.

This component is necessary for setting milestones and following up on the progress of critical issues. To "keep the flame burning," Bekaert uses a variety of other tools. Surveys of workers are used to gauge the level to which *they* think progress is being made. "TQM visits" by management to business units or plants keep the focus of problem solving on key processes and, therefore, key goals. "You start with mutual listening," Decaluwé says. "You give people the opportunity for feedback and they get a clearer sense of direction and progress.

"I was a firm believer after my previous experiences that a team comes up with better answers than an individual; therefore, if you can involve a team in that sort of thinking about strategy, your commitment from the group, having contributed to it, will be far larger and will make the implementation easier. I would certainly stand by that. So it starts from a philosophy of a CEO. In my own view you must feel that, yes, you are CEO, but you also realize that as one individual, given the size of the company, you're in no way physically capable of managing and directing strategy and all the operational issues yourself. So I recognize my own limitation from a physical and intellectual point of view as my starting point on building an organization with a team. In that context, I have found the strategic thinking approach extremely helpful.

"As for the advantages of the strategic thinking process, I was really looking for something that would force our people to think and come up with some answers," says Decaluwé. "It did bring us much closer and the team definitely functioned much better. It gave us consensus. It led us to focus on a few critical issues. We started out with a long list and got it down to five. It led the whole group to take on ownership. On top of that, it is applicable to any level. Not only can you do it for the group, you can do it for business units.

"I call it a 'do-it-yourself kit' for managers in terms of starting to think about where you are with your business and taking hold of it.

"The last two and a half years have not been easy, but it has been a tremendously rewarding experience."

4

Strategic Thinking: The Essence of Competitive Advantage

As noted in Chapter 3, the majority of CEOs we surveyed placed their companies in the Christopher Columbus School of Management—that is, in the quadrant characterized by operational competence but strategic uncertainty. Intrigued, we started looking into the barriers, obstacles, and impediments that prevent companies from operating in the upper-left quadrant, the ideal one to be in. To identify the various obstacles, we went back to these companies to find out how they were run by their CEOs.

Obstacles to Strategic Thinking

We noticed very quickly that people who run companies spend a lot of their time in meetings of one kind or another. My friends at 3M, for example, tell me that when people are appointed "managers," they spend 80 to 90 percent of their time in meetings talking and talking to one another! In many companies, these people have been meeting and talking for years.

The Strategy Suffers from "Fuzzy Vision"

It would seem logical, then, for people in management to have a shared and clear vision of what lay ahead for their organizations. However, when we asked them to describe what their company might look like in the future, we got very different pictures. Each person gave us a distinct version of what that "look" would be (Figure 4-1). That led us to our next question: "What do they talk about?" And what do you think we saw them talk about during all these meetings?

**Obstacles to
Good Strategic Thinking**

Figure 4-1. Strategies can suffer from fuzzy vision.

Management Is Engulfed in Operational Minutiae

Right! They talked about operational issues rather than strategic issues (Figure 4-2). This means that the "look" of the organization starts being shaped by outside forces. And there are many outside forces that will gladly take over the strategy and direction of your company if you abdicate your right to do so yourself. These forces include your customers by the nature of demands they make on your organization—those that you respond to and those that you do not.

OPERATIONAL

STRATEGIC

Figure 4-2. Operational minutiae block strategic thought.

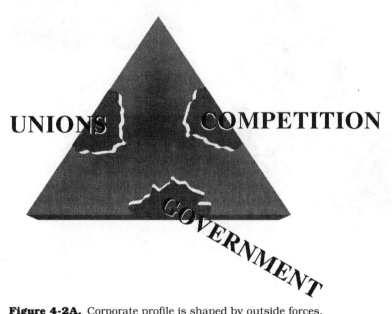

Figure 4-2A. Corporate profile is shaped by outside forces.

No Crisis, No Strategy

We further observed that when times are good, and all the charts, graphs, and numbers are going through the roof, managers have other things on their minds than asking themselves: "Where is this business going?" (Figure 4-3).

Only in times of crisis, when resources become scarce and limited resources must be allocated more carefully, does the need to think strategically surface. Our view is that strategic thinking is an ongoing process during good times and bad times. In fact, if it is held off until the bad times, it obviously becomes more difficult to do.

Figure 4-3. Good times put off strategic thinking.

No Formal Process

The most important obstacle to sound strategic thinking that we discovered was the lack of a formal process (Figure 4-4). Periodically, we would come across a well-intentioned management team that said to itself: "Let's go up to the mountaintop for a weekend and discuss where this business is going." People would then make their way to the retreat, sit around a table, put their elbows up, and start looking at each other. After seven minutes of silence, one of them would finally ask: "Now that we're here, what do we do? Where do we start?" After another seven minutes of silence, guess what kinds of issues they were discussing again? Right! Operational issues—the very issues they didn't want to discuss in the first place.

Figure 4-4. Strategy depends on a formal process.

Even well-led and well-managed companies—including such clients as Caterpillar, 3M, and Dow Corning—did not have a formal process to help them decide what they wanted to become in the future. This observation led DPI to concentrate its efforts and research on the answer to a simple question: "If there is a process to help a company determine its future, what is that process?" In other words, "What questions should people be asking themselves while they are sitting around a table, and in what order should they go through these questions?"

Therefore, when we work with a client, we bring the *questions* and we guide the management team through these questions in a structured and systematic manner. Again, however, it is their *input* going into the process and it is their *output* coming out of the process. This gives the management team complete and absolute ownership of the strategy. As noted earlier, a strategy that has been created by the people who have a vital stake in the future of an organization gets implemented much more quickly and much more successfully than one that is imposed on the organization from outside.

Strategic Planning Does Not Strategic Thinking Make

The 1970s saw the advent of strategic planning as a key tool proposed by consultants to aid corporate managements in determining the future of their organizations. Most strategic planning systems, however, relied on historical data—numbers—that were generated internally. These systems required long and exhaustive analyses with a heavy numerical base. The result was an extrapolation of history into the future. The skill required: *quantitative analysis.*

Strategic thinking, on the other hand, incorporates an assessment of both the internal and external environment. The data are highly subjective and consist of the personal perceptions of each member of the management team. Most of the data are stored in each person's head. The key is to tap into that knowledge base and bring these perceptions into an objective forum for rational debate. The process involves a qualitative evaluation of the business and its environment and is both introspective and extrospective. The skill required: *qualitative synthesis.*

During the 1970s, when strategic planning was at its pinnacle, an avalanche of books appeared under a variety of titles: *Strategic Management, Corporate Strategy, Strategy* THIS, and *Strategy* THAT. Because of my experience in marketing positions at the time, I was attracted to many of these books and started browsing through them to gain a better understanding of what strategy meant.

As I started going through these books, I made two very quick discoveries. First, every author who mentioned "strategy" assigned the word a different meaning. One author claimed that strategy was the *goal* and that operations was the *tactic.* The next author insisted that the goal definition was wrong. Rather, the goal was the *objective* and strategy was the *means.* The next author defined strategy as *long-term planning* and tactics as *short-term planning.* Needless to say, I became more and more confused as I read.

The second discovery I made was that all these books were written by academics who ensconced themselves in business school libraries before posing the question of the century: "What has made General Electric so successful?" And without ever speaking to anyone at GE, but strictly by observing organizations from the outside, they concocted the "miracle" recipes that these so-called winning organizations had used. They then published books extolling their "findings."

We at DPI decided to do our research in a very different manner. We said to ourselves: "Let's go and talk to *real* people who run *real* organizations and ask them how they go about deciding the future of their companies." And we did just that. We started interviewing CEOs in a variety of different-size companies in a variety of different industries in dozens of countries. Eventually, we even sat in on meetings that these CEOs had with their management teams while they were discussing "strategy." Therefore, the concepts described in the remainder of this book are not "miracle" recipes pulled out of the sky. Rather, they represent a process that was extracted from the heads of *real* CEOs running *real* companies.

The CEO's Vision: The Cornerstone of Corporate Strategy

As we started talking to CEOs, we noticed that within minutes they began speaking of a certain "vision" they had for the future of their companies (Figure 4-5). Frequently, what a CEO envisioned his or her company to "look like" in the future was somewhat different from what the company "looks like" today (Figure 4-6).

Figure 4-5. The CEO's vision.

Figure 4-6. A new "look" for the future.

What Is Strategic Thinking?

Creating a vision is akin to painting a picture. Warren Buffett, the renowned investor and founder of Berkshire describes it this way: "Berkshire is my painting, so it should look the way I want it to look."

In view of the above, we came to describe strategic thinking, as opposed to strategic planning, as the kind of thinking that goes on in the heads of CEOs and the key people around them as they attempt to transform their vision into a *profile,* or *picture,* of what the company will "look like" at some point in the future (Figure 4-7).

Figure 4-7. The strategic profile actualizes the vision.

They then would "hang" that profile, or picture, up as a target for all their plans and decisions. Ideas that fit inside the "frame" of the profile were pursued, while those that did not were abandoned. In other words, that profile, or picture, became the "filter" for all their plans and decisions (Figure 4-8).

Why would a CEO want to design a profile for the future of the company? The answer is simple: to ensure that people make consistent and intelligent decisions on behalf of the company. Which leads to the next question: "If I want my people to make good decisions on my behalf, what do I paint inside that picture to help them do that?" Or, "How does the profile of a company transform itself into tangible or physical elements?" Or still, "What elements of a company could I touch or feel that would be tangible evidence of its strategy and direction?"

Figure 4-8. Target for all plans.

How does the company's profile, which is the result of its strategy, reflect itself in physical terms?

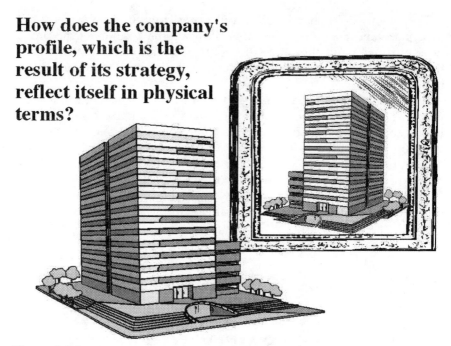

Figure 4-8A.

Inputs and Outputs

To this question, there are several answers. I could look at the company's portfolio of current and announced products. That would be one "clue." I could look at its facilities to see what they produced and where they were located. That would be another clue. I could look at its base of customers and where they reside—its geographic markets. I could examine its competitors and its suppliers. These are other clues. Gradually, as I look at each "piece" of the company, the "puzzle" starts taking shape in my mind as to what that organization will "look like" in the future.

- Products
- Facilities
- Technology
- Talent
- Customers
- Suppliers
- Industry segments

- Distribution methods
- Geographic markets
- Production capabilities
- Competitors
- Selling methods

The "look," or profile of a company that is the "result" of its strategy resides in four of the areas listed above (Figure 4-9). Specifically, the profile of a company finds itself in the nature of

- The products that the company decides to offer
- The customers to whom it offers these products
- The industry segments that it decides to pursue
- The geographic markets that it seeks

All the other elements listed above are either *inputs* to this profile or *outputs* from this profile.

Figure 4-9. Key content areas of the strategic profile.

In order for a profile to give *clear* direction, however, it needs to go a step further and embrace the following content (Figure 4-10):

- Not only the nature of products that will be offered but, more importantly, the nature of products that will *not* be offered.

- Not only the types of customers to concentrate on but, more importantly, the types of customers not to concentrate on.

- Not only the industry segments to pursue but, more importantly, the industry segments not to pursue.

- Not only the geographic markets to be sought but, more importantly, the geographic markets not to be sought.

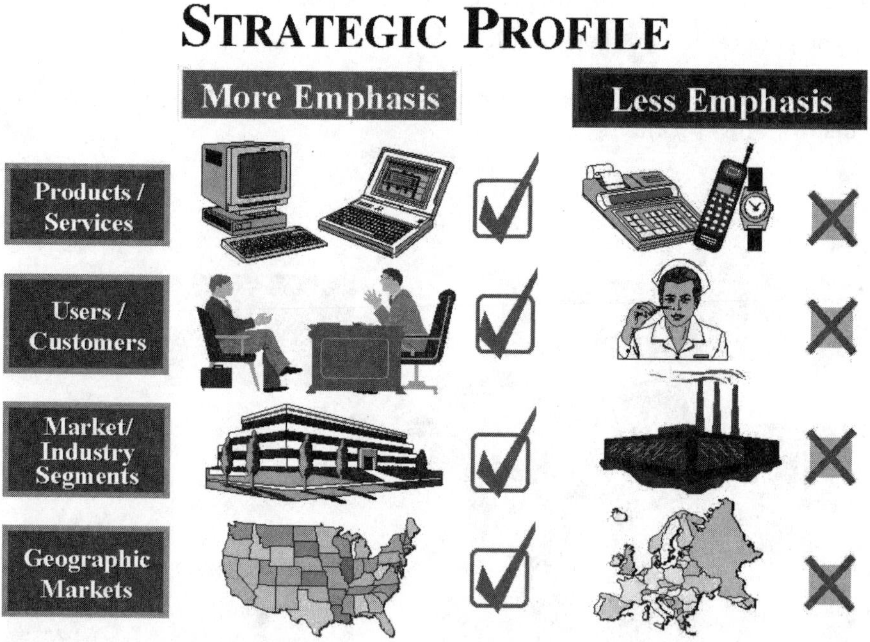

STRATEGIC PROFILE

Figure 4-10. Strategic content includes areas of greater and lesser emphasis.

The Strategic Profile Becomes a Filter for Decision Making

Why should a CEO's vision be transformed into a strategic profile of products, customers, industry segments, and geographic markets to emphasize and, conversely, those to deemphasize? The answer is to create a filter that will help employees make *consistent* and *logical* decisions on behalf of the company. And there are two types of decisions that will shape the "look" of the company over time.

The first is how resources are allocated. Most companies allocate resources through a budget mechanism. The difficulty with most budget systems is that they start at the lowest levels in the organization and creep their way up different silos. How the people at the lowest levels go about determining what they will accomplish in the next two or three years is by looking back at what *they have achieved in the last two to three years*—the numbers—and then projecting the numbers into the future while making minor adjustments for costs, inflation, and currency swings. This type of planning seeks to go forward by looking in the rear-view mirror. It does nothing to change the "look" of the company. Basically, it takes the company in its current state and extrapolates that state into the future.

The primary use of the strategic profile, then, is as a tool to ensure that people in the company allocate resources *strategically* around the organization. With the strategic profile in place, resources are allocated to items that look like those on the *more emphasis* side of the ledger rather than items that look like those on the *less emphasis* side.

The second type of decision that will shape the "look" of an organization over time is how opportunities are chosen. Once the profile is in place, the CEO can send a message advising the troops to pursue opportunities that look like items on the *more emphasis* side rather than opportunities that look like items on the *less emphasis* side.

How a company allocates resources or chooses opportunities are the two types of decisions that will determine the "look" of the business over time. Which brings us to the next question: "How does management go about deciding on the line of demarcation between the items that should receive more emphasis and those that should receive less?" The answer to this important question lies in a fundamental concept of strategy: the driving force.

FirstRand Limited

Looking for Ways to Change the Rules

Laurie Dippenaar
Chief Executive Officer

Even Horatio Alger would be impressed.

In the late 1970s, two men set out with $10,000 and in less than 20 years parlayed that investment into a world-class company with a market cap of nearly $5.5 billion. To make the accomplishment even more stunning, they didn't do it in one of the usual places—Silicon Valley, Wall Street, or some Internet meteor. They worked their magic in South Africa, a relatively small country beset for years by internal strife and external economic pressures.

They did it, the CEO says, by consistently looking for ways to change the rules in their markets and exercising a combination of fiscal savvy and an entrepreneurial management style.

The two original partners were Laurie (pronounced *Low*-ry) Dippenaar and G. T. Ferreira. A third partner, Paul Harris, joined them a year later. All are in senior management with what is now known as FirstRand Limited, with Laurie Dippenaar as CEO. FirstRand is reported to be the largest financial services organization on the African continent. But these men have never forgotten their small company roots.

"We started out offering finance to public utilities for their capital equipment with $10,000 in the bank," Dippenaar remembers. "Now I promise you, you can't compete with that amount of money and those resources unless you've changed the rules of the game *completely*. And that's what we did over the years and we've stuck to that."

Becoming a Price Maker

The idea that got them started was a unique opportunity in a tax break offered to public utilities by the South Africa Tax Act. Says Dippenaar, "There were tax incentives for capital investments in public utilities, but of course the utilities couldn't take advantage of them directly because they don't pay taxes. So commercial leasing companies could come into these deals as participants, and then be able to enjoy a part of the tax allowances. We weren't the only ones to get into this, but we did it a little differently than anyone else. Normally, participants in these deals were advisers who would go to a bank or another finance company, tell it how to structure the deal, and share the profits. But we were brave enough to quote as a principal, a very important difference. So we were able to control the distribution of the profits to the participants. We *made* the price instead of being a price taker.

"Obviously, to accumulate capital either you take capital from outside or you generate it yourself through earnings. We did that by simply using a structure that nobody else had used, and it took time for our competitors to cotton onto what we were doing."

Profits from this stratagem enabled the group to build its initial investment into an expanding portfolio of financial services over the next few years. The company grew quite rapidly.

"We started with this idea of residualizing capital equipment for public utilities," Dippenaar relates. "And then seven years later, in 1984, we acquired control of a small merchant, or investment, bank called Rand Merchant Bank. We grew that to become one of the preeminent merchant banks in South Africa. Our next milestone was in 1992, when we acquired control of Momentum, the fifth-largest life insurance company in South Africa. It was ailing when we bought it, and it took us five years to turn it from an ailing situation into South Africa's most admired insurance company. And then in 1998 we acquired joint control of one of the four biggest banks in South Africa, First National Bank, and also the fourth-largest insurance company, Southern Life. In between these big takeovers, we grew our existing business really rapidly and started a number of new businesses, "seedlings" as we call them. We believe we're quite good at starting new businesses from grass roots. In fact, we make very few acquisitions, but when we do make them, they're extremely large. Our group now covers virtually every facet of financial services. In banking we do commercial banking, investment banking, private banking and finance. In insurance we have life insurance, health insurance, property insurance, and casualty insurance. We're also in fund management and mutual funds. Our market capitalization currently makes us the largest financial services group in South Africa. Just before the July–August meltdown in world financial markets last year, for a brief spell we were South Africa's largest listed company.

"Not large perhaps by American standards, but we are probably the largest financial services group in Africa today."

Dippenaar and his partners have become widely known for a decentralized management structure that encourages prudent innovation and outside-the-box thinking. At Momentum Insurance, for example, they changed its monolithic structure, breaking the company into profit centers so that profit could be measured in small units, not as massive net numbers. Creating an "owner-manager culture," as they call it, produced very successful results at Momentum.

As Dippenaar explains the concept, "One of our core philosophies is that we try to break up big groups into smaller units. We refer to it as 'chunking.' We are great believers in not having monolithic structures. Instead of having a battleship, we prefer to have a hundred destroyers. Even if it's a large market, we believe in doing that. We like lots of captains commanding, with minimal input from the center. That's part of our philosophy. It's really born out of our history. Because we started as a very small company, we still have a lot of faith in the small company mentality. At the same time, we seek out the benefits of a large company balance sheet. So often our legal structure will be one balance sheet and a lot of entities operating with different brands within that legal structure."

Discussing the role of the central management group that binds these independent units together, Dippenaar refers to the management team as the "foxhole at the top."

"We didn't use any other management style except the one where you place a great deal of trust in your own people, because that's the only one we knew," he says. "Those were our roots. So we, almost by accident if you will, applied that management style to Momentum, the first insurance company that we took over. And we just found the people responded very well to it. It unleashed creativity—people being held accountable, being trusted.

"At the top we don't have a command-and-control mentality. We rather see ourselves as being strategic enablers and facilitators. That's the role.

Because we feel that, if you really believe in an empowered, autonomous, owner-manager type of culture in your operating company, the only way to fit in well with that at the center is to style yourself as a strategic enabler and facilitator. We like to think of ourselves as, not a "rule-driven" group, but a "value-driven" group. I explain this to people as follows: Do you want to establish a rule for everything for your children, or do you just want to give them a set of values and then they conduct themselves according to that value system rather than by reference to the rule that father and mother have lain down? This filtered down to all levels and we found ordinary people doing exceptional things."

Bottling the Success Formula

In early 1997, a year before Rand Merchant Bank and Momentum took over Southern Life and First National Bank, the company was brimming with organic growth. It was time, the founders said, to step back, arrive at a clear definition of strategy, and gain an understanding of that strategy across these many units—in effect, to extract their success formula and "bottle it."

At the time one of the traditional management consulting firms was being considered for the job. But it just happened that one of Rand's executives was sick in bed and picked up *Strategy Pure and Simple,* a predecessor of this book. He recognized the strategic thinking process it described as a natural extension of the participative style of management Rand had cultivated. He showed the book to the CEO when he returned to work.

"I was quite pleased about it," Dippenaar recalls. "Normally you would think this kind of thing would come from the chief executive. I was delighted that it came from a guy in sort of second-tier management. I thought it was quite telling for the group that we all had the openness of mind to say, 'Let's try this.'

"In our first exposure to DPI's process," Dippenaar explains, "we actually used it to get the captains of our different operating units, the CEOs, to arrive at a common understanding of our business philosophy. So, it wasn't really what the DPI process was primarily designed for. We weren't trying to necessarily find our driving force, as DPI puts it. But we just thought that if we go through this process we're going to get common understanding and buy-in for our business philosophy. And it definitely achieved that objective. Obviously, what's affected us more than anything else is the fact that the DPI process systematically extracts the thinking and ideas from our executives' heads, rather than imposing the consultant's thinking. I think it almost *forces* ideas out of their heads. That obviously leads to the strategy being owned by the company, rather than by the consultant. I'm not just repeating what DPI says; it actually works that way."

The strategic thinking process with this group and subsequently with various FirstRand units was facilitated by an international team of DPI partners: Rex Glanville of South Africa and Mark Thompson of the United States. Senior executives from the various operating units were able to reach a common understanding of the unique structure and management culture that the company had been practicing and cultivating for nearly 20 years. In such a decentralized structure, particularly one involving a number of acquisitions, there is always the danger of disconnects between the central management's philosophy and objectives and those of the operating units. One way to avoid that is by living the values from the top, and certainly part of the CEO's job is to continuously reinforce the code of goals and beliefs across the many units. But, as Dippenaar found out, those efforts are far more effective if the people in charge of those units have arrived at the conclusions themselves, developing ownership in them and conviction about their importance.

"Remember our objective here was to get an alignment of thinking from executives in the group," says Dippenaar. "Of course we have this decentralized process or 'chunking,' because we'd rather have a hundred companies than one big one, but we need to be sure they're all heading in the same direction. Alignment of thinking is very, very important. And DPI's process is extremely useful for that. You can use it to align thinking within a business unit or you can use it to align thinking within a group of businesses. And it takes hold very quickly. You can get to the same alignment of thinking over years, but with this, in a matter of days you get there. At the time we used it, we had bought and started a number of new companies. It was extremely useful for them to acquaint themselves with each other, and get familiar with what the whole group was all about.

"Now we're not great users of consultants, I must tell you. Consulting firms have a great deal of talent and intellectual depth in them. Often, simply because of that inherent strength in consulting firms, any strategic plan or strategic thinking is *their* thinking, and ownership of that plan or thinking is never embraced by the company. So if there's no ownership, there will be no implementation. In fact, implementation of the strategic thinking is even more important than the thinking and planning itself. If the company does not own the plan, implementation has almost no chance at success, and you've wasted your money.

"Now we've started using DPI's process not just for getting a common understanding and buy-in on our business philosophy, but also for getting the individual companies to identify their driving force and develop plans of their own. We're now using it extensively for the purpose for which it was originally designed.

"As I said, we've never been great users of consultants. Can I just say that it's a credit to DPI that we've used them so extensively? It was partly because the style suits us. We don't want our business run by consultants."

Creating Advantage by Changing the Rules

With its key managers now firmly on the same wavelength, FirstRand continues to search out ways to innovate in all its key markets by looking at them from its unique viewpoint. Dippenaar and his team are convinced that changing the rules—the concept that gave them their start—has been the secret of their success for 20 years and will continue to be.

To bring home the point, Dippenaar gives an example from the insurance business. "In our life insurance company we saw a big swing away from traditional life insurance investment products to unit trusts, or mutual funds. Clearly, at that stage in the industry, life insurance companies regarded mutual funds as enemy number one. We just identified that the market was moving that way. At the time, our life insurance company had a 5 percent market share. So we moved into what we call the mutual funds packaging industry. It's packaging different mutual funds into groups of funds. We moved into that early, well ahead of our competitors. That's a new game in town as an alternative option to life insurance—investment products at the upper end of the market, not the lower end.

"We're great believers that when there's a paradigm shift, when the rules of the game change, everybody goes back to zero. And if you go back to zero, the race starts again. It's the same as if you had 80 percent of the telex market, and faxes come along. You may have 80 percent, but its 80 percent of nothing. The race starts all over again. In our new game, we went to 25 percent market share in just a few years. Companies that, collectively, had a 60 percent market share of the traditional life insurance market now have only 25 percent of the packaged unit trust market, which is a big swing. Originally they had 60 percent, and we had 5.

"The shift, or the balance of power as it were, is just dramatic. We *thrive* on that. We *thrive* on these situations. And we are *alert* and *watch* for ways that the rules of the game are changing."

FirstRand has found that DPI's strategic thinking process has helped it differentiate among opportunities and identify those with the best strategic fit. "One of the most valuable contributions to our thinking from the DPI process is that it provides a filter for the opportunities that you're swamped with," Dippenaar observes. "You can easily choose the ones that fit strategically so you don't go chasing hares across the plains.

"This last merger that we did is now just a year old. Part of the rationale was to take full advantage of this convergence that we see taking place between the products of banks, insurance companies, mutual funds, and fund managers. In recognition of that we've put together a group that has, as wholly owned subsidiaries, all these components. We'd like to think that in the next four to five years, we may rewrite the rules of financial services companies in South Africa. And maybe if we rewrite the rules here, there will be a few other countries that will sit up and take notice."

5

Driving Force: The DNA of Strategic Thinking

The best way to determine if a CEO and the management team have a strategy is to observe them in meetings as they try to decide whether to pursue an opportunity. When we sat in on such meetings, what we observed was that management would put each opportunity through a hierarchy of different filters, but the ultimate filter was always whether there was a fit between the products, customers, and markets that the opportunity brought and *one* key component of the organization. If they found a fit there, they would feel comfortable with that opportunity, and would proceed with it. If they did not find a fit there, they would pass.

Different companies, however, looked for a *different* kind of fit. Some companies looked for a fit between the products. Others were less concerned about the similarity of products than about a fit with the customer base. Still others were interested, not in a fit between products or with the customer base, but rather a fit with the technology involved, or the sales and marketing method, or the distribution system. Some quick examples.

What fit was Daimler looking for when it bought Chrysler? Obviously, the fit was one between similar products. Johnson & Johnson, on the other hand, looked for an entirely different kind of fit when it acquired Neutrogena creams from one source and the clinical laboratories of Kodak, dramatically different products. The company was looking for a fit between the class of customers served—doctors, nurses, patients, and mothers—the heartbeat of J&J's strategy. 3M looked for still another fit when choosing opportunities. 3M did not care what the products were or who the customers were; what 3M did care about was whether there was a fit between the technology that the opportunity required and the technology—polymer chemistry—that lay at the root of 3M's strategy. If the technology fit, then 3M management felt comfortable in pursuing that opportunity.

Ten Strategic Areas

The next question that came to our mind was: "What are the areas of an organization that cause management to decide how to allocate resources or choose opportunities?" We discovered that each of the 300-plus companies we had worked with consisted of ten basic components:

- Every company offered a **product** or **service** for sale.
- Every company sold its product(s) or service(s) to a certain **class of customer** or **end user.**
- These customers or end users always resided in certain **categories of markets.**
- Every company employed **technology** in its product or service.
- Every company had a **production facility** somewhere that utilized a certain amount of **capacity** or certain in-built **capabilities** in the making of a product or service.
- Every company used certain **sales** or **marketing methods** to acquire customers for its product or service.
- Every company employed certain **distribution methods** to get a product from its location to a customer's location.
- Every company made use of **natural resources** to one degree or another.
- Every company monitored its **size** and **growth** performance.
- Every company monitored its **return** or **profit** performance.

Two Key Messages

As a result of these observations, two key messages emerged. First, all ten areas exist in every company. Second, and more importantly, *one* of the ten areas tends to *dominate* the strategy of a company consistently over time. It is to favor or leverage this one area of the business time and again that determines how management allocates resources or chooses opportunities. In other words, one component of the business is the *driving force* of the strategy—that company's so-called DNA. This driving force, in turn, greatly determines the array of products, customers, industry segments, and geographic markets that management chooses to emphasize more or emphasize less.

The Driving Force As the Strategic Engine

In order to explain this concept more clearly, let's look at an organization as a *body in motion*. Every organization, on any one day, is an organism that has movement and momentum; it is going forward in some direction. Our thesis is that the *driving force*—one of ten components—of a company's operation is the strategic engine behind the decisions that management makes (Figure 5-1). Some typical examples follow.

What determines which products we offer, which markets we seek, and which customers we attract?

Figure 5-1. Defining the driving force.

Strategy Driven by Product

A company that is pursuing a product-driven strategy has deliberately decided to limit its strategy to a singular product and its derivatives. Therefore, all future products will be modifications, extensions, or adaptations of the current product, and the current product is a linear, genetic extrapolation of the very first product that company ever made. In other words, the look, form, or function of the product stays constant over time. Examples are Coca-Cola (soda), Boeing (airplanes), Michelin (tires), Harley-Davidson (motorcycles), and many of the automobile manufacturers (GM/Toyota/Volkswagen).

Strategy Driven by User or Customer Class

A company that is driven by user or customer class has deliberately decided to restrict its strategy to a describable and circumscribable class of end users or customers (people). And those end users or customers are the only ones the company serves. The company then identifies a common need of the user or customer class and responds with a wide array of genetically unrelated products. Examples are Johnson & Johnson (doctors, nurses, patients, and mothers), AARP (adults over 50), Playboy ("entertainment for *men*") and USAA (military officers).

Strategy Driven by Market Type or Category

A company that is driven by market category has deliberately decided to limit its strategy to a describable marketplace or market type. The company identifies a common need among buyers in that market and then responds with a wide variety of genetically unrelated products. Examples are American *Hospital* Supply (now Allegiance) and Disney's concept of "wholesome entertainment for the *family.*"

Strategy Driven by Technology

A technology-driven company is rooted in some basic, hard technology such as chemistry or physics or some soft technology such as know-how or expertise. The company then goes out looking for applications for its technology or expertise. Once it finds an application, the company develops a product that is infused with its technology for that application, and offers the new product to all the customers in that market with a similar application. While growing that business, the company goes around looking for another application to repeat the same process. Examples are Dupont (chemistry), 3M (polymers), and Intel (microprocessor architecture).

Strategy Driven by Production Capability or Capacity

A company driven by production capacity has a substantial investment in its production facility. The key phrase heard around the company is "keep it running"—three shifts per day, seven days per week, 365 days per year. The strategy is to keep the production facility operating at a maximum level of capacity. Examples are steel companies, refineries, and pulp-and-paper companies.

A company driven by production capability has incorporated some distinctive capabilities into its production process that allows it to do things to its products that its competitors have difficulty duplicating. As a result, when the company goes looking for opportunities, it restricts its search to opportunities where these capabilities can be exploited. Specialty converters in a variety of industries are good examples.

Strategy Driven by Sales or Marketing Method

When a strategy is driven by sales or marketing method, the company has a unique or distinctive method of selling to its customers. All the opportunities it pursues must utilize that selling method. Examples are companies that sell door to door (Avon, Mary Kay, and Amway), direct-response companies (Dell and K-tel), and catalog companies (L. L. Bean and Land's End). A recent addition is Amazon.com, whose strategy is to use the Internet to sell a wide array of consumer products.

Strategy Driven by Distribution Method

A company driven by distribution method has a unique or distinctive approach to moving tangible or intangible things from one place to another. All the opportunities such a company pursues must optimize that distribution method. Examples are Wal-Mart, FedEx, Home Depot, Staples, and Nextel.

Strategy Driven by Natural Resources

Companies whose entire purpose is the pursuit and exploitation of oil, gas, ore, gold, timber, and other resources can be said to be pursuing a natural resource-driven strategy. Examples are Exxon, Shell, Newmont Gold, and Anglo-American Mining.

Strategy Driven by Size or Growth

A company driven by size or growth is usually a conglomerate of unrelated businesses. Its sole strategic interest is growth and size for their own sake.

Strategy Driven by Return or Profit

A company whose sole strategic focus is a minimum level of return or profit is typically a conglomerate of unrelated businesses. The best example during the 1970s was ITT under Harold Geneen. His dictum of "an increase in quarterly earnings, every quarter, from every unit, regardless of what" led ITT into 276 different businesses. These businesses were deliberately kept separate so that when any one unit missed its profit target for three consecutive quarters, it was gone in the fourth! Other examples today are AlliedSignal and General Electric, where Jack Welch's dictum of an 18 percent ROA has landed GE into everything from light bulbs to television networks to financial services to turbines.

Key Strategic Questions

When we take a client through our strategic thinking process, we have the CEO and the management team debate three key questions.

> QUESTION 1: Which component of your business is currently *driving* your strategy and has made you look like you look like today in terms of current products, customers, and markets?

If there are ten people in the room, how many answers do you think we get? Right! Ten and sometimes more. The reason is simple. Each person has a different perception of which component of the business is the driving force behind the company's strategy. These different interpretations lead to different visions of where the organization is headed. The difficulty, while this is going on, is that each member of the team is making decisions that pull the company left and right, so the company zigzags its way forward.

The methodology we bring to bear at DPI encourages management to look back at the history of decisions they have made and, by doing so, to recognize a pattern. Typically most of their decisions were made to favor *one* component of the business. Thus, the management team comes to recognize the *current* driving force behind their *current* strategy.

> QUESTION 2: Which component of the company *should be* the driving force behind the company's strategy in the *future?*

This question is more important, because it focuses on the future. A company's future strategy should not be an extrapolation of its current strategy. Rather, the strategy needs to accommodate the environment that the company will encounter in the future, and that environment could be very different from the one encountered in the past.

> QUESTION 3: What impact will this driving force have on the choices the company must make regarding future products, customers, and markets?

Which driving force the company chooses as an engine of future strategy will determine the choices its management makes as to the products, customers, and markets that they *will* and *will not emphasize.* These choices shape the profile of the company over time. Each driving force carries different choices that will make the company look very different from the way it looks today. In other words, your personal DNA determines what you look like and why you look different from other people. The same is true for your corporate DNA. What area of the company you choose as the DNA of its life will determine what that company will eventually look like and why it looks different from its competitors.

An example, again, is Johnson & Johnson. A few years ago, the managers of J&J's Philippines division noticed that young Filipino women used its baby talcum powder to freshen their makeup and carried a small amount in a handkerchief to use when they were away from home. The Filipino managers saw an opportunity and they developed a "kit" that consisted of a holder for the powder together with a mirror and a powder puff. They then created an advertising campaign aimed at this segment, and they opened new distribution through supermarkets and drugstore cosmetics counters. When corporate headquarters in New Jersey got wind of the project, Filipino management was sent a terse directive to cancel the project. "We're not in the cosmetics business" is all the memo said. Filipino management had forgotten that J&J is in the business of satisfying the *health* needs of *doctors, nurses, patients, and mothers* and not the cosmetics needs of young, probably single, women.

The Fundamental Concept of Strategy

The concept of driving force—to us at DPI—is one that is *fundamental* for any successful CEO to understand. It is the recognition and understanding, by all members of the management team, of that *one* predominant component of the business, its DNA, that will allow the organization to formulate a strategy based on a *distinctive* and *sustainable advantage* that can make competition irrelevant.

Getting agreement on a single driving force is not an easy task. The following questions raised by CEOs and their management teams reveal the reasons why.

Does Your Strategy Suffer from the "Sybil Syndrome"?

"I can think of four or five strategic areas present in our business and they are of equal importance." In other words, there are *multiple* driving forces at work in the company. When we present the concept of driving force to CEOs for the first time, this is usually the first response that we get. We call it the "Sybil syndrome." Do you remember the movie *Sybil*, about a woman with multiple personalities? Every morning, she awoke without knowing who she was. The same can be true of a company.

If multiple strategic areas are at the root of a company's strategy, and these strategies are regarded as equally important, the organization will develop multiple personalities and won't be able to tolerate itself. The following strategy statement, from a real company, is a good example:

> The Corporation strives to be a profitable and growing global manufacturer and marketer of value-added chemicals, an innovative supplier of niche life insurance and annuity products, and an increasingly significant force in the pharmaceutical industry.

The company? The Ethyl Corporation. When was the last time you saw this company mentioned as a super performer? In fact, the company had such difficulty living with itself that it eventually divided into *four* separate public companies.

Does Your Strategy Suffer from Schizophrenia?

"If there cannot be multiple business areas driving our strategy, then I can identify two components in our company, equally important, that work in tandem." We call this the "schizophrenic strategy." One day you are in *this* mode, the next day you are in *that* mode. And the company zigzags its way forward, bouncing from one questionable opportunity to another.

Our contention is that, at any one moment in time, every organization has a single business component that is the driving force behind its strategy. Until members of the management team determine which component that is, they will have frequent disagreements over the allocation of resources and the choice of sound opportunities to pursue.

Is Profit Not the Single Purpose of a Company?

It is a well-known fact that people must eat in order to survive. If they don't eat, they will die, guaranteed! But surely the purpose of life is not eating. Surely, there must be another purpose to life other than eating, although people must eat everyday.

The same line of thinking applies to a company. Most businesses have another purpose in life, a driving force other than profit, although whatever that driving force is, every strategy must produce a profit. If a company is not profitable, it will die, guaranteed! However, profit is the *result* of the strategy, not its *objective*. Profit tells you whether your strategy is working or not, but profit is not usually *the* strategy.

Isn't Any Strategy Subject to Darwinism?

Doesn't every strategy evolve over time? In other words, doesn't a company start with a certain driving force and evolve naturally to a second driving force and then eventually to a third, and so forth? Could you not start as a product-driven company and then become technology-driven and then customer class–driven? Isn't there a natural evolution over time?

The answer, generally, is no. A good strategy stays in place and works for an organization over a long period of time. Take, for example, Mercedes' concept of the "best-engineered car." This strategy was first articulated in 1888 and, from then until today, that concept has produced a profit every single year. The same is true of Wal-Mart, Johnson & Johnson, Disney, and several others. In fact, we would propose that the opposite is also true. If you feel that your strategy needs to change frequently, that is a clear signal you don't have one!

Are There Any Legitimate Reasons for Changing the Driving Force?

There are two instances when you might want to shift the strategy and direction of your organization by deliberately changing the underlying driving force of your current strategy.

The first occurs when your current strategy runs out of growth. Growth, like profit, is a "given" in business. Any company must grow to perpetuate itself. Therefore, when your strategy starts sputtering and runs out of growth, you have a *legitimate* reason to sit down with your team and debate whether the time has come to change the historical driving force behind your current strategy. One company that has been in this mode for the last ten years is Playboy. Its long-time strategy of providing "entertainment for men" with a very specific profile (young adult male, single, middle to upper income) led the company to everything from magazines to casinos. The strategy worked for 30 years. However, in the 1980s, the absolute number of young adult single males began to diminish as a result of evolving demographics, and Playboy's strategy started running out of growth and came to a quick halt. Since then, Playboy has been looking for a strategy that will prove as good as the one that worked for over 30 years.

The second situation arises when you look down the horizon and see a death threat. In other words, there is something at the root of the company's strategy that could make the current driving force obsolete. This is another, extremely *legitimate* reason for calling a meeting to explore changing the strategy and direction of the company. Such might be the case for a company like Johnson & Johnson. If anyone—that is, anyone other than J&J—ever invented a *wellness* pill, that would be the end of J&J's strategy of satisfying the "health needs of doctors, nurses, patients, and mothers." Then you would see J&J look for other customer groups to satisfy with radically different products than today's. J&J executives, on the other hand, have looked down that horizon and don't see obsolescence as a very high probability, so they will stay with their current driving force and strategy.

Does Your Strategy Succumb to Seduction?

Alongside these two legitimate reasons for changing the driving force and strategy of a company are factors that cause the strategy to change by *accident and not by design*. Opportunities seduce management! An opportunity comes along and management, looking only at the numbers, concludes that it cannot afford not to be in that business. The company then pursues the opportunity, because of the numbers, only to discover later that the opportunity has another driving force at its root. Before long, the opportunity starts pulling the whole company off course.

When Is Seduction at Its Peak?

A company's management succumbs to seduction when its current strategy is so successful that it is generating more cash than the business needs. And the company starts accumulating excess cash. This is a situation that happened to Daimler Benz, as it was known in the mid-1980s. From 1975 to 1985, the company accumulated a cash hoard of over $8 billion—a windfall that had nothing to do with the sale of cars, but rather with swings in the currency markets. Rather than keep the money for a rainy day, the then-CEO decided to go on an acquisition binge; the company soon found itself the proud owner of AEG, Dornier, and MBB—all three in major trouble. Trying to fix these businesses caused management to take its eye off the ball—the car business. The shift in focus gave BMW an opening to concentrate on taking market share away from its main rival, which is exactly what it did. It took Daimler Benz over ten years to dispose of these albatrosses and refocus itself on the car business. The company finally acquired Chrysler in 1998, an acquisition it should have made 15 years earlier, when Chrysler could have been bought for a song.

Are Some Driving Forces Inherently Incompatible?

The answer is yes. A good example is Compaq. During the 1990s, under CEO Eckhard Pfeiffer, the company soared on its product-driven strategy—business PCs. The strategy was so successful that management convinced itself that it could run any computer company. So when Digital Equipment Corporation (DEC) ran into difficulties, Compaq jumped in and bought DEC outright. Compaq quickly discovered that it had acquired a company with a very different strategy—complex information systems for corporations—a concept driven by market category. Instead of being in the relative simple business of selling and distributing personal computers in different-colored boxes, Compaq now found itself in the business of providing large, multitask computers that required proprietary software and ongoing service, elements that PCs don't need. Here were two *very different businesses*—and, unfortunately, two conflicting driving forces and strategies. It doesn't matter how smart management thinks it is: if two strategies are *inherently incompatible,* they will never be made to work.

This conflict turned out to be fatal for Pfeiffer. Six months after the merger became official, the company announced earnings that were 50 percent below Wall Street's expectations. Pfeiffer was quickly ousted by the board's chairman, Benjamin Rosen. At the press conference announcing the dismissal, Rosen stated that "Compaq's strategy is sound. Execution is the hang-up. We need to execute better." Compaq's customers thought otherwise. "I don't know what they stand for anymore" said one. In our view, Compaq had adopted an incoherent strategy. And just as its customers recognized Compaq's strategic incoherence, so did its employees. Thus, the reason for poor execution. People cannot be expected to execute well a strategy that is flawed from the word "go."

Strategy by Design, Not by Accident

The purpose of the strategic thinking process is to help a company's CEO and management team make *conscious* decisions whose rationale and underlying logic are clearly understood. Understanding what the company does best—its strategic heartbeat and corporate DNA—is a key skill of management. Formulating and deploying a distinctive strategy that capitalizes on the company's DNA and that can be leveraged to the company's benefit to lock in markets and lock out competitors is the CEO's next challenge.

3M Company

3M

Two Decades
of Strategic Thinking

Mike Harnetty
Division Vice President

What products immediately spring to mind when you think of 3M? Post-It® Notes? Scotch® Tape? Fluoromaterials? It would probably come as a surprise to most people that the company they associate with some of the most useful consumer products ever made also makes a wide array of much more obscure, yet profitable products—like fluoromaterials.

"These are specialty materials," explains Mike Harnetty, who heads up the 3M unit. "It's sort of a specialty within a specialty. We are not a chemical company. We do quite a lot in the chemical business, but these products are an offshoot of a basic 3M technology that was used internally. We had to make this stuff to go into some other products we make, and at some point someone started looking at it and thought, 'Gee, what if we took this outside and tried to sell it to somebody? Do you think we could find anybody who would be interested in it?' We started that 50 years ago. And over that 50 years we've found quite a lot of people who would be willing to pay quite a lot of money for a number of products that we have and things that we can do.

"We happen to have a unique manufacturing process that we developed at 3M over a period of years. It's a very unusual process that would be difficult for any other company to duplicate. That's one reason no one else in the world practices this particular process that we use to make our fluoromaterials. But over the years, we've done quite well by going out and marketing the unique materials it produces, and finding applications for them."

"Who Are Those Guys?"

The division that makes these chemical intermediates was conceived in the 1940s and began commercial production in the early 1950s. For decades the division enjoyed a lone position in a market it essentially created, with no major competitors.

Then serious trouble began to emerge in the late 1970s when several chemical companies that had noticed the potential in that market developed new fluoromaterials products of their own. But complacency was deep in the 3M unit. Many of the managers simply refused to recognize the threat. It seemed impossible to them that after all these years of success, competitors could force them to change. However, several of the top executives were alarmed and realized that without a new strategy, their very survival could be at stake.

"It reminded me of that scene from *Butch Cassidy and the Sundance Kid*," says Mike Harnetty, "when Butch and Sundance are being relentlessly pursued by a posse. No matter what they do they can't shake them. Finally, Sundance looks at Butch and says, 'Who *are* those guys?' That's the way we felt. Who *are* these guys disrupting our comfortable world?"

Some in the group recognized the seriousness of the situation and realized that it was imperative to bring in outside help to craft an urgently needed new strategy. But that conviction was by no means universal.

Says Harnetty, "At the time the feelings were all over the map about this. There were people who thought that we could just do what we always did—go out and sell, sell, sell. Ignore the competitors. There was an Italian company, a couple of Japanese companies that we didn't know. Some people didn't take them seriously. But there were also some people who took this very seriously and thought we'd better start planning. Some thought that developing strategy was just a little too sophisticated for us—after all, we're a smokestack business. Let's just go back and grind it again, sort of a 'hit it with a bigger hammer' approach. It was not unanimous among our group that we could sit down and think our way through future planning or strategic thinking."

But the need *was* clear to the president of the group at the time. Having encountered DPI's strategic thinking process, which had been used successfully elsewhere at 3M, he decided that this approach would be the best way to make everyone understand the problem—and the immediate need for change.

As Harnetty, who was national sales manager at the time, recalls, "The boss just said, 'Go ahead and do it.' He was trying to get us away from this myopic, internally focused, close-to-the-vest way of doing business. He was the kind of guy who was always after us about the fact that someday we'd have to encounter the real world, the competition. And when that happened we'd have to deal with it or shut it down, one of the two. So it came down as an order to be at a certain place at a certain time for two or three days to talk about strategy. Nobody knew much about the DPI process, but we went ahead."

However reluctantly, the leaders of the manufacturing, "inventing," and sales and marketing groups gathered offsite to see where the DPI process would take them. And where it did take them was through a complete strategic review of every key aspect of the company's business.

"This was really our first exposure to trying to look at our business strategically," Harnetty says. "We had 30 years of experience in a market-leading position. It was a small business. It was fairly well isolated from the real world. It had very much of a specialty flavor, and it was very protected. We didn't have to worry much about competition. There was no one else doing what we were doing, either directly or indirectly. We didn't have to worry about the rest of the world. What we were really trying to do was protect our world. We just wanted somebody to verify that we were right, and if we could just keep doing what we were doing, we'd win. That's what we were looking for when we came into this meeting."

Separating Fact from Myth

But that's not what they found. In fact, the group began to see a very different picture as the DPI process systematically elicited the facts from their heads. It wasn't easy, but some entrenched beliefs were brought out and openly discussed, separating fact from myth.

"What I specifically remember about that first encounter with the DPI process is that it generated a lot of debate," Harnetty says. "Underneath the surface, we all had different ideas, different levels of concern. Some people felt, very strongly, that we were already on the right track and didn't have to change. And others thought, 'No, we're very vulnerable.' It certainly provided a forum for those kinds of differences. I've got to say the DPI process was responsible for bringing those ideas out. But I think, as much as anything, it was Mike Robert's ability to generate argument, to allow these differences in thinking or feeling about our business and our vulnerabilities or strengths to come to the surface. We wrestled with them, got them out in the light and fresh air, sorted them out, and figured out how to deal with them.

"The DPI process was very, very effective for us. This was partly because we were not an organization that wanted some consulting expert to come in and tell us how to do our business. We were extremely successful at it. We knew it better than anybody. What we needed was a facilitator, or a referee, to get the argument started, get the juices flowing, let people say what they thought, and then put a process on the table that allows them to think all of that through and deal with it. Then you aren't going home with everybody firmly entrenched in *their* thinking, with nobody's mind changed at all."

Gradually, Harnetty and the 3M team thrashed out the details of the emerging competitive environment, and came to the undeniable conclusion that these marauders were real and they weren't going away. It also became clear that if they didn't make the necessary changes, these outside forces would decide their fate.

"When we began to see that there was a competitive environment there, it was obvious that we were no longer isolated, protected. We were in the arena and there were people all around watching. We needed some understanding of how to compete. What were the rules? How could we win? We knew there were competitors on the field. Our next task was obviously to determine our strengths and weaknesses. We needed to find some way to offer additional value by means of some unique strength," says Harnetty.

The debate then centered on determining which of the ten driving forces was at the crux of this unusual business. All other decisions would be a direct result of that most crucial one. "It was quite obvious to some of us, and in later sessions to the rest of the crew too, that Mike Robert was not there to provide answers, but more clearly, I suppose, to provide us with a process to discover our own answers. And that worked. No one else was inventing this for us. It was ours.

"In that whole discussion, probably the single biggest discovery was this driving force concept. What is your driving force? *What is the one thing?* Your driving force is the one thing you do better than anyone else, or the one thing that makes you unique. And identifying that driving force led us to the conclusion that that's what we needed to protect.

"We found our driving force to be our 'process' *technology*—this unique manufacturing process that no other chemical company could begin to understand to the degree that we do. But we understood it, and it worked for us. Because of that, because no one else was ever likely to pick it up and deal with it, we said that's what makes us different. How can we use that? And from that point on, from that day in 1980, we began to think of how we could utilize this uniqueness to evaluate our strengths and weaknesses, to look at our competitors and find our competitive space. In the 20 years since then we've spent a lot of time continually trying to define that competitive space—the place where we have a better chance of winning than anyone else.

"Also, at the end of the session and subsequent sessions, the DPI process gave us a chance to consider potential priorities. Now that we're in this enlightened state, what are the top five things that will give us the greatest chance of winning? So, I guess that was the most important thing about the DPI process. At the end of the session I think we would have said that what we'd been through was a process of self-discovery, again—strengths and weaknesses, our place in the competitive market, a greater awareness of the competitive threat. And like that scene from *Butch Cassidy and the Sundance Kid,* we discovered that there were competitors back there chasing us. We were suddenly asking ourselves: Who *are* these guys? What are they trying to *do* to us?"

From Theory to Practice

To ensure that the strategy would become a reality, several critical issues were agreed upon, then brought to fruition over the next several months. Among them was an evaluation of their entire line of products, applications, and customer groups.

"One of the things it did was to segment our business," Harnetty says. "We had a portfolio of products, businesses, and markets. We had always treated them all the same. They were all wonderful. They were all good. We could just chase them all and not worry about it. One conclusion the DPI process brought us to was that we needed to begin prioritizing those businesses, and evaluating the opportunities they presented in the light of our driving force and our competitive threats. This led us, very early on, to decide to get out of some businesses. There were two or three businesses that we were in for reasons that nobody could remember other than, 'We're in them so we've got to participate in them.' And it laid the groundwork for some decisions soon after that. We said, 'Here are four or five businesses or product lines that we should not be in.' The reason was that they were not connected to our driving force. We had no real business being in them. We couldn't protect them. We couldn't be better than anybody else at them. And also, someplace along the line, it dawned on us during one of the DPI sessions that we had only so much energy in the enterprise. And we could disperse it so a hundred different projects get 1 percent of our energy—in which case, none of them has much energy. Or we could circle the wagons, pick out five of the best opportunities, and give each of these 20 percent of our energy. Now they have a much better chance of surviving. And we're going to be much smarter about them. If your plate's too full, you've got to throw something out.

"And we actually began to do that, cast off businesses, either sell them or, for the most part, shut them down. The payoff was getting rid of these secondary businesses and building up the primary businesses that we wanted to protect."

To make a long story much shorter, the group went ahead and cut those businesses loose—and thus survived. In fact, it has grown to be a very substantial business for 3M. 3M's fluoromaterials group has, in the course of time, developed a very sophisticated understanding of their market position. And they have worked with DPI to revisit their strategy every three or four years to keep it sharp.

"Today, for example, I would say that we now divide our business into three or four major opportunities that are described more by the external market than they are by us," states Harnetty. "We now look at the total market and say, 'What is our share in it?' One of the things that we found was that if you describe your business narrowly enough, you always have a very good market share. And in that tiny little world, you are the king. Well, if you can step back and look at the larger market, you can keep describing your market until you have no more than a 5 or 10 percent market share. Now what does that market look like? And since you have described a market that is so big, related to you, what are your opportunities within that market?

"We have gotten to that point. We are very, very comfortable with that now. We are looking at a market that is several billions of dollars, and we're seeing our tiny little piece here of about $1 billion. But we're saying, within that market of, say, $8 billion, where are our other opportunities? Where could we go, again focusing on what we're good at, the driving force? And one of the things that this has led us to, as we keep evolving and using DPI's process that we started 20 years ago, is a new skill to adjust our vision and lose a little of this internal focus to think more externally. In fact, I'd say we're probably one of the leading organizations within 3M to begin to get out and look at partnering. Maybe take in other people's products and market them, or do joint development projects."

The 3M fluoromaterials business is now building on that concept, looking at ways to expand on its driving force to move beyond the division's current capabilities and limitations.

"When we came out of that original strategic thinking session, we said, 'We have this one driving force, that's what sustains us, that's what we have to protect.' And that energized us and got us going. But having been there for 30 years, and seeing this thing develop, I can now say that it is a pretty dynamic situation. We have found subsets of that driving force, other things that we can do well, recognizing that this one is at the heart. But if you look long enough you will see other things emerging that we are good at, maybe combining our driving force with others in our own business. Or more importantly today, if I look at my driving force or at what I'm really good at, I then start looking at other people in the specialty materials industry, and say, 'How can we take what we're good at, combine it with what you're good at, and create a new one that didn't exist before?'

"All of that may sound new, but I can trace it all the way back to that original 1980 meeting, at least for me personally. That is, you'd better understand what your strength is, focus on what you're good at. If you're not good at anything, then you've got to question why you're in this business. But if you're fortunate enough to find something that you're unique at, have a better chance of winning than anyone else, then that's what you build on. That becomes the cornerstone of the business. And all your strategy should flow out of exploiting that, or protecting it. It gets to be pretty simple in a hurry actually. But then when you start to look at combining your strength with others, and creating a new capability together that is unique, that's what's leading us into some of this partnering or joint venturing. That's going to be the major change for our business, creating new opportunities for growth in the twenty-first century."

6
Crafting and Articulating a Distinctive Strategy

If you were to browse through the annals of business history books, you would learn from author after author that, on any one day of its existence, every organization practices a *concept* of conducting its business. In other words, there is an *underlying concept of business being practiced by the management of that organization at any moment in time*. Thus, an organization's business concept is synonymous with what we have described as its strategy. In my mind, these two terms—"business concept" and "strategy"—are one and the same. There are many business "historians" who share this view.

Alfred Sloan, the creator of modern-day General Motors, said it this way in his 1972 book *My Years with General Motors*:

> Every enterprise needs a concept of its industry. There is a logical way of doing business in accordance with the facts and circumstances of an industry, if you can figure it out. If there are different concepts among the enterprises involved, these concepts are likely to express competitive forces in their most vigorous and most decisive forms.

Henry Mintzberg, a well-published authority on the subject of strategy, made a similar observation in a 1980 *Harvard Business Review* article:

> Strategy is the organization's conception of how to deal with its environment for a while. If the organization wishes to have a creative, integrated strategy . . . it will rely on one individual to conceptualize its strategy, to synthesize a "vision" of how the organization will respond

to its environment. A strategy can be made explicit only when the vision is fully worked out, if it ever is. Often, of course, it is never felt to be fully worked out, hence the strategy is never made explicit and remains the private vision of the chief executive.

The guru of all management gurus, Peter Drucker, calls it the "theory of the business." He outlined his thesis in a 1994 *Harvard Business Review* article:

> Every organization, whether a business or not, has a *theory of the business*. Indeed, a valid theory that is clear, consistent, and focused is extraordinarily powerful. These are the assumptions that shape any organization's behavior, dictate its decisions about what to do and what not to do, and define what the organization considers meaningful results. These assumptions are about markets. They are about identifying customers and competitors, and their values and behavior. They are about technology and its dynamics, about a company's strengths and weaknesses. These assumptions are about what a company gets paid for. They are what I call a company's *theory of the business*.

We at DPI concur and endorse the three views expressed above. We call it the organization's *business concept* or *strategy*. We also view as synonymous *mission, charter, mandate, business purpose,* or any other such term that expresses an organization's *raison d'être—its reason for being.*

In our view, the *driving force* is the organization's reason for being. Identifying the organization's future driving force is a tool available to help management isolate the one component of the business that will be at the root of the company's future products, customers, and markets. The *business concept* is a description, by management, of how it plans to employ and deploy that driving force as a strategy to deal successfully with the environment the organization will face and provide a distinctive and sustainable advantage against the competitors it will encounter.

Unfortunately, in most organizations the business concept or strategy is implicit and resides in the head of the chief executive. Other people find out what the business concept is by the nature of the decisions that are accepted or rejected over time. Depending on the recommendations that are accepted or rejected, people slowly figure out what the strategy is and where the line of demarcation is between what the strategy permits to be pursued and not pursued in terms of products, customers, and markets. The result of an implicit strategy is, however, that these people may guess wrong as often as they guess right.

Many CEOs, therefore, find it imperative eventually to make their strategy *explicit* and put it into hard copy. Doing this, however, can prove to be a more difficult task than they expected.

The Futility of Meaningless Mission Statements

For over 20 years, we have made it a practice of collecting "mission statements" that various organizations have published as instruments to give them a sense of direction and as tools to empower employees to make intelligent decisions on their behalf. What we have collected over that span of time could give Dilbert enough material to last a lifetime.

We will refrain from embarrassing some well-known corporations by attaching company names to the mission statements that follow. Still, these excerpts demonstrate why we refer to them as *meaningless* mission statements. Try to determine what business the company in this first example is in.

> We are a successful, growing company dedicated to achieving superior results by assuring that our actions are aligned with shareholder expectations. Our primary mission is to create value for shareholders.

Given this statement, the company could be in any business on any given day. Here is a second example.

> Our mission is to provide products and services of superior competitive quality and value, to achieve strong growth in sales and income, to realize consistently higher returns on equity and cash to fuel our growth, and to have people who contribute superior performance at all levels.

What business is this company in? Again, any business it wants to be in. In fact, these two companies could be considered to be fierce competitors. Here is a third example.

> Our primary enterprise objective is to increase the value of shareowners' investment by managing our resources and servicing our customers better and more efficiently than our competitors.

What an industry! We've never encountered a business with this intensity of competition. These mission statements, although well intended, serve no purpose whatsoever. One person who expressed well the futility of such statements was John Roche, a GM vice president:

> A bunch of guys come into a motel room for three days, take off their coats and ties—put a bunch of nice-sounding words on a flipchart—and go back and do things as usual.

Why do we refer to these as meaningless mission statements? The reason is simple. They are statements put together by well-meaning executives using nice-sounding words that can get everyone to nod in agreement. However, when such statements are used as filters to help people make intelligent decisions, they fall apart because they allow everything through. Typically, people make several attempts at using the mission statement as a filter for decisions, only to uncover its shortcomings. They then quietly file the statement away in the bottom drawer, where it never sees the light of day again, and go back to business as usual.

The Usefulness of a Meaningful Business Concept

In their zeal to give the organization a sense of direction, many CEOs succeed instead in giving it a sense of delusion. After witnessing the frustration of CEOs in attempting to articulate their strategy, we at DPI developed the following guidelines for crafting a meaningful business concept—one that helps people make intelligent decisions on behalf of the company.

- The first line of the statement must clearly describe the one component of the business that will be the *driving force* of its strategy.

- The remainder of the statement should describe how management will deploy the driving force in a manner that clearly delineates the line of demarcation between the products, customers, and markets that the driving force lends itself to and, by deduction, those that it does not.

- The statement should have a "tone" of growth, since a company must grow to perpetuate itself. The statement should have a "tone" of success, since any viable strategy should breed success.

- The statement should reflect *future intent* and not present condition. It should articulate what the organization intends to become and not what it is today.

- The statement must result in the articulation of a distinctive strategy that gives the organization an advantage over its competitors—an advantage that will grow over time and, hopefully, lock in markets and lock out competitors.

Altogether, the statement should be one paragraph, two sentences, in length. Why not any longer? Simply because we have learned from experience that the ability of people to execute a strategy statement is inversely proportionate to the length of the statement. In other words, the longer the statement, the less likely the strategy will ever be deployed successfully. The reason is simple. People cannot remember!

A good strategy statement, then, must be short, clear, and succinct. Further, each word must be chosen very carefully, since it will move the line of demarcation one way or another as to what the strategy permits and does not permit.

Real Business Concepts

The following are examples of real business concepts drawn from real companies—namely, our clients. We have deliberately chosen examples that have guided corporate actions for more than five years. We did so to demonstrate the lasting power of a sound strategy. We have also chosen examples that are representative of each driving force so the reader can see the nuances. In each case, the description of the driving force appears in italics. We have kept the statements anonymous, since many of the companies are well known and do not wish their strategy to become public knowledge.

The first two business concepts are from product-driven companies— one in the manufacturing sector and the other in the service sector.

Our vision and strategy is to remain the global leader and prime innovator of *cushioned slippers* that serve the comfort needs of people indoors or around the home in countries with a lifestyle that encourages the purchase of such footwear.

Our strategy is to provide *reinsurance products* that assist organizations manage life, health, and annuity risks. We differentiate ourselves by applying our superior mortality/morbidity risk management expertise. We concentrate on growth-oriented customer segments located in "free" geographic markets with reliable databases and predictable risk patterns that will bring a balanced portfolio.

The next two concepts are driven by user or customer class.

Our strategy is to proactively seek out the information management needs of *operators of turbine-powered aircraft*. We will respond with differentiated products and related services that leverage our proprietary database in market segments and geographic areas with multiple customers.

Our strategy is to fulfill the complete spectrum of health care needs of *cancer patients* and respond with holistic treatment options that truly "make a difference," delivered by the ablest professionals in a seamless and sensitive manner that empowers patients to make coherent decisions. We will concentrate in geographic areas where we can be involved with all the constituencies in the continuum of cancer care.

The following is an example of a concept driven by market category.

Our strategy is focused on the professional information and education needs of the *health science market*. We will provide added-value content that maximizes the development of valuable copyright materials through multiple formats, languages, and/or distribution channels to reach multiple customer segments.

A strategy driven by production capability might look like this:

Our strategy is to exploit our superior *wire pickling and drawing capability* in the pursuit of high-volume opportunities and to respond with better-performing products that meet the needs of customers in the garment processing industry in geographic markets where our plant locations bring an additional advantage.

Then there is the concept driven by production capacity:

Our strategy is to market transportation fuels to *optimize our refining capacity*. We will seek high-volume customers in geographic areas where our distribution outlets provide a competitive advantage.

The next two statements are examples of technology-driven concepts:

Our strategy is to enhance our leadership position in *specialty alloy technology* to address high-tolerance performance requirements of customers located in geographic markets within reasonable proximity of our technical centers.

Our strategy is to leverage our proprietary *screen vibration technology* to satisfy the separation of solids and liquids for applications that result in differentiated products with superior performance at acceptable cost for customers in geographic markets where we can provide technical support.

Now for a concept driven by sales method:

Our strategy is to become the largest retailer of a wide range of financial products using the *Internet as our sales method* to reach adults with substantial investment, tax, and capital preservation needs residing in any geographic market that can be reached electronically.

A concept driven by distribution method is our final example:

We will be the premier owner/operator of an *international wireless network* that provides point-to-point, two-way communication with multiple users for companies with large numbers of mobile workers located in major urban centers of industrialized countries.

Exotic? Definitely not. Sexy? Absolutely not. Powerful? You bet! The purpose of a clear business concept is not to arouse people but to provide them with a clear sense of direction and equip them with a simple, but extremely effective tool to make intelligent and consistent decisions on behalf of the organization when allocating resources and choosing opportunities.

The Business Concept as a Strategic Filter

The following statement is the business concept of another one of our clients.

> Our strategy is to leverage our *multipurpose, continuous-process* capability to combine metals and polymers to produce and market multilayered structures for applications where we can respond with unique products that add value, are tailored to the specific needs of end users, and bring cost, quality, or performance advantages. We concentrate in growth-oriented industry segments and geographic markets with multiple applications.

Although a bit wordy and somewhat technical in nature, this statement can be converted into a very simple, but powerful binary filter to quickly screen opportunities that come to the business. The filter is created by transforming the business concept into a series of questions that require a yes or no answer. Table 6-1 shows how the statement above would look in a binary mode.

Table 6-1. Strategic Filter

Does the opportunity . . .	Yes	No
Leverage our multipurpose, continuous-process capability to combine metals and polymers?	☐	☐
Produce *multilayered* structures?	☐	☐
Result in a differentiated product that adds value?	☐	☐
Result in a product *tailored* to the specific needs of the customers?	☐	☐
Bring: • Cost advantages? • Performance advantages? • Quality advantages?	☐ ☐ ☐	☐ ☐ ☐
Target a growth-oriented industry segment?	☐	☐
Reside in a geographic market with multiple applications?	☐	☐

The more "checks" that the opportunity receives on the no side of the ledger, the larger the red flag should become, because that opportunity violates major elements of the strategy that is at the root of the company's existence. The more negative checks that the opportunity receives, the less likely the company will be able to pursue that opportunity successfully. The opportunity is an exception to the rule, and exceptions always turn out to be major problems.

Too many companies assume that its personnel know what business the company is in and what the strategy is. This is the assumption that results in "meaningless" mission statements and decisions made by accident rather than by design.

FLEXcon, Inc.

FLEX con

Making the Strategy Stick

Neil McDonough
Chief Executive Officer

$100,000,000. Eight zeros. For some of today's megacompanies, a $100 million year may not seem like a lot. For FLEXcon, based in Spencer, Massachusetts, reaching that figure in 1986 was an important milestone, one the company had been working toward for 30 years.

As FLEXcon president Neil McDonough recalls, "My father started the company in 1956, and it took ten years to grow it to $1 million. It took another ten to grow it to $10 million in 1975. So from that point we had it as a long-held goal to get to $100 million and do it in ten years. When we got there in 1986, the whole company gave a sigh of relief. There were celebrations and congratulations. But there was no sense of what we should do from there."

Then director of marketing, McDonough and the rest of the management team were looking for a way to create new goals for the company and a means to reach them. In other words, they were looking for a way to develop a growth strategy to take FLEXcon to the next level, whatever that would be.

"I happened to read *The Strategist CEO*, Mike Robert's first book," says McDonough. In it he came across a description of the strategic thinking process. He immediately recognized it as the means for FLEXcon's managers to leverage their knowledge and experience, creating a strategy together. He passed the book along to CEO Myles McDonough and then-president Mark Ungerer, who agreed they should give the process a try. "It was obvious this was what we needed to help us understand our future direction."

So DPI was brought in to take FLEXcon management through the process, and today McDonough sees it as a critical turning point in the company's history.

In McDonough's estimation, the company had been very strong from an operational standpoint, but lacked the future vision it needed. The strategic thinking process changed that for good. "As a company," he says, "we always had a cultural sense of our strategy. We could describe ourselves as a pressure-sensitive films manufacturer. We had always done a pretty good job of declining opportunities that would drift us away from that. But we didn't have a good sense of what we needed to do to grow our core strength.

"We were very department-oriented. Although we had monthly staff meetings, they tended to be presentations from the departments, not discussions of where we were going in the future. It became very difficult to do new things. Each idea had to be sold to the people who would implement it. But once we went through the strategic thinking process, any new ideas were, in effect, presold. The result was that everything was easy to accomplish if it was part of what we said our strategy would be. Everybody was on board, no explanations needed."

The strategic thinking process enabled management to agree on a driving force and a better definition of what FLEXcon would be and become. As McDonough describes it, "Deriving from the strategic thinking process, our driving force is technology and know-how. Around here we talk more about the know-how than the technology because everybody thinks technology is high tech. The know-how is combining a customer's applications needs with our coating and laminating and film selection know-how, or material development expertise, to make a product that works on that application. Given that as our core strength and our driving force, it leads us into so many different areas."

Changing the Rules—Just in Time

In 1987, not long after FLEXcon finally reached its $100 million milestone, a serious threat suddenly emerged. A Japanese company bought a coating company just down the road. It quickly became obvious to FLEXcon managers that the new group would be going after their market aggressively.

"So we went through a mini-strategic thinking process," McDonough remembers. "We said, 'If we wanted to go after the heartbeat of our business, how would we do it?'—particularly if we used Japanese manufacturing strategies. We were producing all our products on a custom basis, hundreds of them. We always thought it was a great strength to provide that kind of variety. But if I were going to compete against us, I would come out with a few standard products that had superior quality and consistency of performance, price them low, and get UL approval—which for us is like the Good Housekeeping seal of approval. So we decided we'd do it before the Japanese had the chance. We knew that the company they had bought didn't have the equipment to compete with us yet. But the rumors in the industry were that they immediately ordered the equipment so they could go right after us."

FLEXcon management sat down and hammered out a plan in mid-January to launch by April, whittling down 168 products to a dozen standard products that would meet all the customer needs then served by all those custom products. They were priced to make it very difficult or impossible to underprice FLEXcon profitably. The company planned the production to run on two of its newest machines and geared up quality teams for zero defects.

Mark Ungerer believed that if the new competitor was successful, FLEXcon could lose more than 20 percent of its sales almost overnight. "We weren't about to let that happen," says McDonough. "They were about to change the rules of play on us, so we went full out to change the rules on them."

McDonough, then in his marketing role, carefully designed the program to avoid cannibalizing its own products and set prices to thwart countermoves. "The pricing ended up being 20 percent under the pricing for the custom equivalent. I learned from Procter & Gamble that customers will not switch to an unknown product unless they see at least a 20 percent advantage in pricing. In our industry it takes about a 10 to 15 percent difference to cause the customer to switch.

"So the program was set to launch in April. We used DPI's potential problem analysis to look for things that might become obstacles later, and decided that resistance from the salespeople might be a problem. They're compensated on dollar volume, not units."

In anticipation of those objections from its own salespeople, McDonough placed an ad in trade journals with the new price list. Three weeks before the ad would run, he announced the new program to the sales force. "We told people they had three weeks to look like heroes with their customers," McDonough recalls. "We said, 'Go out there and hit every customer. Make sure everybody knows.' "

The program was a huge success. The new competitor was caught flat-footed. By the time the Japanese company had a product line the following September, it was too late. "The fact that we were able to develop the idea in January and launch the product in mid-April without a hitch shows how well the strategic thinking session worked. You think of all the time it takes for a brochure to be printed, for data sheets, not to mention setting up the manufacturing and getting approval from UL. It was an amazingly tight time frame.

"Not only did we not cannibalize existing lines; we got a ton of new business. Customers started coming to us with significant pieces of business. Business that had gone to lower-priced competitors started coming back to us. Two major competitors got out of that segment of our business, and the new competitor never really got going, although it's still around.

"It was from this that we started talking about ourselves as our own best competitor. Now we offer the best competitive choice, within one house, of short custom runs or standard products. Two entire product lines came out of the new manufacturing capabilities we had learned. The Eveready battery business we have today, we wouldn't have thought we could take on efficiently. The whole glass bottle business that we developed, we wouldn't have thought we could take it on and develop it. If we hadn't realized this threat and moved swiftly to change the rules in our market, we'd be a much different, much smaller company," says McDonough.

Growth Continues

In the ensuing ten or so years, FLEXcon has charged ahead. Sales have swelled to over $350 million, a new plant has been added in Scotland to serve the European market, and products now range widely from labels for shampoo and wine bottles to membranes for touch pads and holographic security indicia. Yet these products all stem from FLEXcon's agreed-upon driving force—its specialized know-how in the development of adhesive-backed materials. And strategic thinking as well as other DPI critical thinking processes has become an important part of the culture.

As McDonough remembers it, "For the first three years or so after we went through the process, our way of applying it as a decision-making filter was not as formal as what we've done since then—which is to take our business concept and turn it into a literal filter of yes or no answers to seven or eight questions. Back then, all we had to do was describe an opportunity in terms of what we had said in the strategic thinking session and make a decision on that basis.

"Today, when we're evaluating each situation such as developing a new product, we're looking at strategic fit and ease of implementation. To determine the strategic fit, we have taken our business concept, two paragraphs long, and turned it into eight simple yes or no questions, such as

'Will this bring us closer to the customer?' 'Will this allow us to fragment the market?' 'Will we bring new materials to this application?'

"It's not a matter of right or wrong," he continues, "and you don't have to have a perfect yes on every single one. It just gives you the tools to compare various alternatives. If you've got one with six yesses and two nos, and another one with two yesses and six nos, it doesn't take a genius to know which one to pick.

"The other thing this approach does is force people to ask those questions, and it opens up the idea to challenges. It enables us to say not just whether it will bring us closer to the customer, for example, but how. It puts all those issues on the table. It takes the idea beyond someone's opinion and allows open questioning."

McDonough also recognizes that even the best strategy needs to be evaluated on a regular basis. He feels that the right time frame for his business in its particular environment is six years for a complete review of the strategic thinking process, with a "quick gut check" every three years. "We've gone through the full-blown process actually three times, with different numbers of people. These sessions haven't led to any changes of direction. What they have allowed us to do is to really refine our business concept, make it better and more clearly delineated."

FLEXcon management has even engaged in strategic thinking from the standpoint of its competitors. "By putting ourselves in our competitors' shoes, we got a much better understanding of how they may react to any given situation. They have different strategies and different driving forces than ours." In McDonough's pocket, next to his company's business concept card, is another card that carries his competitors' concepts, better enabling him to anticipate future competitive moves.

"The real value in revisiting the strategy on a regular basis is not in changing direction, but in getting our business concept more and more refined, understanding our situation better, and developing the list of critical issues to bring us closer to that vision that we've got for our future," McDonough states.

At DPI, critical issues are initiatives that must be accomplished in order for a strategy to succeed. Having a strategy is one thing; getting it done is another. The disciplined management of these critical issues drives the deployment of a successful strategy.

Ask Neil McDonough what FLEXcon's critical issues are, and he knows them off the top of his head. So do his key managers. "The critical issues are blended into our monthly staff meeting," he explains. "Each is broken out into small assignments. Each has a key champion responsible for it. It's never been a problem of people neglecting those issues because these people are all a part of coming up with the agreement that those are the key issues."

Critical Thinking Processes— Part of the FLEXcon Fabric

Over the past ten or so years, the people at FLEXcon have worked with Mike Robert and DPI partner Craig Bowers to embrace a full range of critical thinking processes developed by DPI. These processes provide a common framework, and logic pathways for evaluating various kinds of opportunities, problems, and decisions in a rational, disciplined manner.

DPI's decision-making processes embrace such components as decision analysis, problem analysis, and potential problem analysis. At FLEXcon, these processes are applied to a wide range of decisions. "When we have a decision to make we automatically use decision analysis, and we use problem analysis and potential problem analysis all the time. It's become a part of the way we do things. In fact, I used to require a decision analysis worksheet on any capital expenditure of $10,000 or more. I then found there were a lot of $9000 decisions being made, so we've changed our approach on that. But we consider these processes to be a very important part of our business. They're part of the common language around here," McDonough states.

DPI's Continuous Process Improvement® and Business Process Improvement® are used to apply these logic tools to the challenges of evaluating, optimizing, and improving the manufacturing and administrative processes within the organization. FLEXcon has used them to achieve exceptional levels of quality, efficiency, and cost control.

Because employees have not only the authority but the tools to make decisions, it is visibly apparent that this is an exceptional company. As one visitor to FLEXcon's facilities recently said, "When you walk into the plants, you can see immediately how well run they are. These are plants handling all kinds of adhesives and you can practically eat from the floor."

The company also uses DPI's Strategic Product Innovation® to direct the use of its new product development resources. Most companies use SPI to continuously search out and evaluate new products, customers, and markets. But FLEXcon applies the process somewhat differently. Because its customers supply a steady stream of new ideas for products, FLEXcon uses the SPI process as a strategic filter to evaluate these many opportunities. "Filtering" each product opportunity by several measures, the company's people are quickly able to make decisions as to which products should be emphasized in terms of timing and resources, and which should receive less emphasis.

As McDonough explains, "Most of our product developments aren't thought up in the lab. They're actually thought up by the customer. We want to respond quickly, and our previous processes were flawed in that they created obstacles to getting things approved and implemented. Now people can quickly evaluate strategic fit, ease of implementation, and cost/benefit, and everybody has the right, if not the obligation, to get working on the project. Approvals now may come as disapprovals and they're usually done by the people involved. They have the tools to evaluate the criteria themselves and can then get access to resources to pursue the project.

"New products are the lifeblood of our company. We put this process into place about 18 months ago. And after 18 months 30 percent of our sales come from new products. We started with a goal of 30 percent in three years. Obviously, we blew that away. Through the first four months of this year, we came up with 179 products, using combinations of materials we had never made before. We made and sold them. So this has been very successful for us!"

Driving Future Growth

As FLEXcon continues to grow, the business concept stays constant, but of course new challenges lie ahead. As part of its goal of reaching $1 billion by 2010, FLEXcon is expanding overseas. Its recently built plant in Scotland is part of that drive. Getting the new staff there on board with the FLEXcon strategy and management methods is key to the success of that new facility.

Says McDonough, "We built the manufacturing facility and hired some key people in Scotland who have not been part of the FLEXcon organization for very long. As a company, we tend to have low turnover and try to promote from within. In our key staff group, I don't think there's anybody with less than 15 years of experience. Then we got over there and didn't have that. They're very bright, capable people, and they understand our business, but I don't believe they'll have it in their blood until they've gone through the strategic thinking process. They'll have their own list of critical issues, yet we still share the same business concept.

"We also need to get them involved in these other thinking processes. One of our managers was over there and some issue came up and he asked, 'Have you done a decision analysis on that?' They looked at him like he had three heads. So we want to get to the point where when there's some issue, major or minor, to talk about, we use the same language. We may not always use the worksheets, but we use the logic we've learned.

"We use these tools for all kinds of operational and strategic decisions. I even used decision analysis when we sat down to work out a corporate structure that will enable the company to grow toward our goal of $1 billion by 2010."

McDonough looks confidently toward that objective with expansion plans into new markets and the further development of the ever-increasing stream of new FLEXcon products. To what does he attribute his company's exceptional focus?

"It all comes down to getting agreement on the driving force, and the business concept, so that you can develop the critical issues from there. It's very straightforward. You've just got to invest the time and do it. And do it with a facilitator who has the experience to force you through these questions and keep the process on track. Then, once you've gotten down to the critical issues, give people the tools to make the right decisions and get things done. If you're going to tackle complex issues, you've got to embed these concepts in your company's culture," McDonough concludes.

$1,000,000,000. Nine zeros. A long jump from eight. Can the company accomplish the goal by 2010? Managers at FLEXcon are not only certain they will; they also have a clear strategy and an action plan to get there.

7
Areas of Excellence: Widening Your Competitive Advantage

As we worked with more and more companies over the years, we started noticing that some companies had a strategy that gave them a distinctive advantage over their competitors over long periods of time. In other words, their strategy worked for many years and even decades. On the other hand, their competitors would go up and down like yo-yos every three or four years. In industry after industry, there is always a small cadre of companies that, regardless what is going on in the environment or on the competitive front, as the commercial says: "They just keep going . . . and going . . . and going!"

One example is Mercedes and its concept of the "best-engineered car." That concept was first articulated by Karl Benz in 1888, and every year for the last 100 years, without exception, the company has made a profit in spite of veering slightly off course during the 1980s.

Wal-Mart is another example. Has there been a recession for Wal-Mart? Apparently not. The company has enjoyed more than 30 consecutive years of 10 to 15 percent increases in revenues and profits. Yet, in a recession, which industry is hit first and most? You're right—retail! Sears, JCPenney, and K-Mart, but never Wal-Mart.

"What is it that these companies know about strategy that their competitors don't or have forgotten about?" we asked. The answer: a concept we came to call *areas of excellence*. In pursuit of the answer, we again went out to talk to the CEOs of these companies in order to understand what they did. What did we discover? The companies that kept their strategy strong and healthy over a long period of time clearly understood that, of all the skills and capabilities they had developed over this time, two or three were more important to their strategy than all the rest of them together. In these two or three skill areas, the company deliberately attempted not only to be more proficient than it normally was but also to be *more proficient than any other competitor in that specific capability.*

Defining Areas of Excellence

We came to define an area of excellence as a *capability* that can be *identified, located, and isolated* and then nurtured to a higher level of proficiency— higher than any other capability the company has achieved and higher than any skill a competitor has attained in that area. It was by being more proficient than any other competitor that the company maintained a strong and healthy strategy, and gained the edge on its competitors. The converse was also true. If the company ever allowed its proficiency to diminish in these areas, then its strategy, like a person, got ill and weak. As the strategy weakened, the company's competitive edge disappeared.

However, we also discovered that there is a direct relationship between the force that drives the strategy of the business and what its areas of excellence need to be. And these areas of excellence, or strategic skills, differ from one driving force to another (Figure 7-1).

Product-Driving Force

Many of the automobile companies—Ford, General Motors, Toyota, Chrysler, Mercedes, Nissan, Fiat, and Volvo, among them—have restricted their strategy to a single product and its derivatives. One way to identify the *areas of excellence* required to succeed in a product-driven mode is to ask: "Who's been winning the car wars in the last 40 years?" The answer is obvious: the Japanese. Ford has held its own, but GM is *half* the company it was and is still losing market share (Figure 7-2).

Why did Americans, Canadians, and Europeans switch in droves from domestic auto manufacturers to Japanese makers during the 1960s, 1970s, and 1980s? The answer is simple: the Japanese made better cars. A product-driven company has locked itself into a single product family, selling that same product over and over again, probably to the same customer over and over again. As such, the bottom line for the success of a product-driven strategy is simple: *the best product wins!*

Figure 7-1. The driving force defines areas of excellence.

The proof is in the pudding. When the first Japanese cars landed on U.S. shores in the mid-1950s, were they "better cars"? Of course not. They were the laughing stock of the industry. However, the Japanese quickly learned that "the best product wins" and they embarked, with the help of Dr. Deming and Dr. Juran, on a 20-year campaign to make their "product" better and better. Today, thanks to the Japanese, a car that doesn't work perfectly from the moment you step into it is unacceptable.

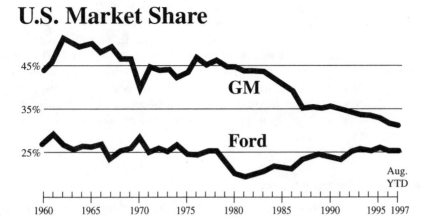

Figure 7-2. Winning the car wars.

A required area of excellence for a product-driven company, therefore, is product improvement, product embellishment, product development, or product enhancement. In other words, making the product better and better is a *key strategic skill*. A product-driven company must do this better and more often than any of its competitors.

Another example is Caterpillar, one of DPI's long-term clients. Over the span of six or seven decades, Caterpillar introduced dozens of innovative earth-moving machines that its competitors could barely imitate and that made Caterpillar the unchallenged worldwide leader. In the late 1960s and early 1970s Caterpillar, basking in its success, made a number of acquisitions that took it outside of its product-driven strategy. To finance these acquisitions, management diverted its resources away from product development. As a result, the "gap" in the performance of Caterpillar's products and those of rival Komatsu narrowed, and Caterpillar's leadership position eroded to the point that by the mid-1980s the company was in a death spiral.

When Caterpillar used our strategic thinking process for the first time in 1988–1989, the major discovery the company made was that by reducing the product development budget, successive managements had given Caterpillar a self-inflicted wound. The new management decided there and then to sell off Caterpillar's unrelated acquisitions and rededicate the company to making "better" products. The product development budget was restored to its traditional levels. The result: an avalanche of innovative products that Komatsu has not been able to keep pace with and that helped Caterpillar regain its global leadership.

A second area of excellence required for a product-driven company is either *sales* or *service*. Caterpillar, again, is a case in point. Caterpillar's machines are found in every country on this planet and, in most countries, in very awkward places. As we all know, machines in the field periodically break down. Caterpillar, through its dealer service organization, can get any machine, anywhere in the world, back up and running within 24 hours—guaranteed. And Caterpillar comes through 99 percent of the time. Strategic capability, area of excellence, and competitive advantage: no other competitor can make this claim. In fact, this was the key capability that sustained Caterpillar through Komatsu's assault and gave Caterpillar the time needed to shore up its product development area of excellence, as mentioned above.

User-Class Driving Force

When a company has restricted its strategy to an identifiable set of end users with a common need, that strategy will succeed only if the company understands its user group's needs better than any of its competitors do. The company must anticipate new or emerging needs from this user class, in advance of its competitors, in order to modify current products or offer new products more frequently than its competitors do. Therefore, upfront *user knowledge* is a key strategic capability.

Johnson & Johnson (J&J) and Procter & Gamble (P&G), two companies driven by user class, conduct interviews or hold focus groups with millions of users annually in order to detect any changes in the preferences, habits, or demographics of these users before their competitors do. As a result, they can adjust their product offering more often than these competitors. This capability is their area of excellence and competitive advantage. By continuously nurturing this capability to higher and higher levels of proficiency, these two companies widen their edge over their competitors.

Another area of excellence for such companies is *user loyalty*. J&J has cultivated a high level of product loyalty on the part of its users by winning their "trust." Users should trust J&J because its products are "safe" for every member of the family. J&J doesn't allow anything to infringe on that guarantee of safety—to the extent that it will remove a product from the market if it even has the smell of being unsafe. Thus J&J recalled Tylenol® some years ago even though the product was being tampered with only in Chicago.

Technology Driving Force

A technology-driven company prospers on its ability to push the envelope of knowledge about the hard technology (e.g., physics or chemistry) or the soft technology (e.g., know-how or expertise), that is at the root of its strategy. It is by enhancing its knowledge in this area that the organization keeps uncovering new applications that lead to a continuous stream of new products. Therefore, *basic or applied research* is a key strategic skill.

A case in point is Pfizer. Until the early 1980s, Pfizer was just an average pharmaceutical company plodding away at the average pharmaceutical industry pace. Then Edmund Pratt, Jr. was appointed CEO. His vision was clear: to make Pfizer the best "prescription drug company in the world"— a technology-driven strategy. From 1981 through 1990, he increased R&D spending from 8 percent of sales to 14 percent, or $602 million. During this period, Pfizer launched nine new "blockbuster" drugs that generated over $2 billion of revenues.

Pratt's successor, William Steere, continued his legacy. His first few decisions were to exit a number of businesses that were not related to this strategy. Out went the talc mine in Montana and the medical devices business. "Distractions," said Steere. He also invested the proceeds from these sales into R&D, tripling that budget in eight years to over $2.2 billion in 1998. The figure represents 18 percent of Pfizer's sales and is substantially higher than that of any competitors. Merck, for example, spent only 10 percent of its revenues in that same year.

Pushing the envelope of knowledge to higher levels of proficiency in certain key areas has produced spectacular results for Pfizer. Several new blockbuster drugs ($100+ million in annual revenues) have already been introduced—including Viagra (impotence), Norvasc (hypertension), Zoloft (depression), and Zithromax (infection)—and the company still has the fullest pipeline in the industry. Over 50 potential blockbuster drugs are in various stages of human trial and can be expected to receive FDA approval in the next few years. Steere's financial results have been even more spectacular than his predecessor's, with 1998 profits checking in at $2.6 billion on revenues of over $13 billion. In eight years, sales have doubled, profits have tripled, and the stock price has increased eightfold!

All this is happening in an era in which Pfizer's competitors are merging and purging and cost cutting without achieving results anywhere close to that of Pfizer. In the meantime, Steere keeps increasing the R&D budget—an area of excellence that he deliberately nurtures to a higher level of proficiency in order to widen the gap over competitors.

CEO Steere is well on the way to realizing his, and Edmund Pratt's, vision of Pfizer as the best prescription drug company in the world.

Production Capacity Driving Force

When a company has a substantial investment in its production facility, a chief concern is uptime ("keep it humming"). In such a mode, the company must focus on two areas of excellence in order to survive and prosper. First, the company must strive to be the *low-cost producer*. During a period of glut, when there is an overabundance of product in the market, the first decision the company must make is to cut the price. The reason is simple: the last decision it wants to have to make is to stop the production facility. Second, if the company wants to survive in a period of glut and low price, it must have the *most efficient production facility* in the industry. Therefore, in prosperous times, profits are quickly reinvested in making that production facility more and more efficient—in anticipation of the period of glut and low prices.

Two good examples of companies that clearly understand the importance of being the low-cost producer as an area of excellence are Mead in the paper industry and AK Steel in that industry. Both companies have enormous investments in their production mills, which, as a result, must be kept running as much as possible (uptime).

In the paper industry, where most companies are losing money, Mead is a noticeable exception. While all its competitors are diversifying into other businesses, Mead CEO Jerome Tatar has focused the company's strategy on being the low-cost provider by concentrating all its efforts on productivity enhancements and cost reductions. And his strategy is working. In 1998 Mead reported earnings of $150 million on close to $4 billion of revenues—the best in the industry.

Another CEO who is widening the gap over his competitors is Richard Wardrop, Jr. of AK Steel. His strategy is also driven by production capacity. "We're crazy bastards about uptime," he claims proudly. With that as a war cry, Wardrop has concentrated the company's efforts on becoming the low-cost producer, a required area of excellence, by reducing the length of the shutdown to reline its furnaces. Abandoning the industry practice of taking four months per furnace every six years, AK Steel shuts down its furnaces only two weeks every two years; thus its furnaces run ten weeks more than competitors' furnaces over that six-year period. Each additional day of production brings in $1 million in operating income. As a result, AK Steel is the most profitable of the six remaining U.S. steel producers. Its operating margin of 12.4 percent is two points higher than the industry average.

Sales- or Marketing-Method Driving Force

Many companies have a strategy driven by a unique or distinctive method to sell to customers. The two areas of excellence required to make such a strategy work are the *reliability of the sales network* and the *effectiveness/coverage of that network*. Dell Computer is a good example. Its network of telephone sales agents is the most productive and easy to do business with of any in the industry. Dell has also been able to extend this customer-friendly advantage to the Internet, where it generates over $10 million per day of revenues.

Distribution-Method Driving Force

FedEx and Wal-Mart are two companies pursuing a distribution-method driven strategy. FedEx's distribution system of small trucks to airplanes to small trucks at the other end will accept any size package that the system can handle. Wal-Mart's distribution system consists of clustering ten to twelve stores around a central warehouse that replenishes these stores on demand. The company has cloned this system all around the country.

A strategy driven by distribution method wins only if it is reinforced by two areas of excellence: *system coverage/reach* and *system efficiency*. At FedEx, CEO and founder Fred Smith said: "The main difference between us and our competitors is that we have more capacity to track, trace, and control items in the system." At Wal-Mart, CEO David Glass described his company's area of excellence: "Our distribution facilities are one of the keys to our success. If we do anything better than other folks, that's it."

Both CEOs have deliberately given these strategic capabilities preferential treatment by investing a higher and higher percentage of their revenues each year in cutting-edge information technology (IT) systems. Over the years, the total has been substantially more than that of any competitor. Each company did so because it recognized that these areas of excellence were required to give its distribution method a sustainable competitive edge. For more than 35 years now, not one FedEx or Wal-Mart competitor has figured this out or, if one or two have, they have not been able to do anything about it.

Natural Resources Driving Force

Successful natural resource-driven companies excel at doing just that—exploring and finding the types of resources they are engaged in. Two companies that have been very successful by cultivating different, but related, areas of excellence are Exxon and Shell.

Exxon has long been recognized by its competitors for its ability to find oil in some of the world's most difficult places. It is this strategic ability that has given Exxon an advantage over its competitors.

Shell's success has come from nurturing a different area of excellence. Shell's particular expertise is "enhanced oil recovery in offshore waters deeper than 8000 feet," a capability that started at 600 feet but that was nurtured over the years by several billions of dollars. The investment was made consciously by several consecutive CEOs who clearly understood Shell's competitive advantage. This advantage has been demonstrated several times with the discovery of some 12 million barrels of oil from tracts so deep that Shell's competitors did not even bid.

Thus, the two areas of excellence for a natural resource-driven company are *exploration* and *conversion.*

Maximizing Size/Growth or Return/Profit Performance

Conglomerates of unrelated businesses often pursue strategies that are driven by financial goals exclusively. One area of excellence is *portfolio management.* This is the proficiency of buying and selling assets in order to maximize the size/growth or return/profit performance of the overall organization.

A second area of excellence is *information systems.* Conglomerates of unrelated businesses usually have a corporate "big brother" group that constantly monitors the performance of its various divisions in order to detect and eliminate negative performance as quickly as possible.

Areas of Excellence Must Be Given Preferential Treatment

A management concept practiced by too many CEOs today says: "Give to everybody and take away from everybody . . . *equally.*" We at DPI have great difficulty with this approach, because it is not strategically sound. In our view, once management has identified the driving force of its strategy, it must identify the supporting capabilities that need to be nurtured toward excellence and then give those areas *preferential treatment.* In other words, in good times, we give key areas more resources than other areas of the business. In bad times, we trim everywhere else but we don't trim these key areas of skill. If we did, our proficiency would diminish, our strategy would weaken, and our edge against our competitors would disappear.

A good example of a company that has come to recognize this fact is Corning. For several decades, Corning was a very successful company that introduced a number of creative products based on its knowledge of glass. In the past decade, however, the company started floundering and saw its financial performance and stock price go into a downward spiral to a low of $23. In 1996 the company appointed Roger G. Ackerman as its new CEO. Ackerman immediately recognized the importance of clearly identifying the company's driving force and then nurturing key supporting capabilities into areas of excellence.

His strategy, based on returning Corning to the innovative applications of silica, which is the technology at the root of glass, called for giving *less emphasis* to its traditional products such as cookware and giving *more emphasis* to new growth applications in photonics, liquid crystal displays, and fiber optics. To realize his strategy, Ackerman also identified the need to excel in Corning's knowledge of silica technology. In other words, his *technology-driven strategy needed to be supported by superior R&D* to push the envelope of knowledge of silica. Ackerman quickly slashed costs across the board—except in the area of R&D. In fact, he increased the R&D budget from 3.4 percent of sales to 8.4 percent for a total of close to $300 million. He also doubled the size of Corning's research facility and increased the number of scientists by 67 percent, to a little over 1500. Finally, Ackerman refused to put his limited resources into a stock buyback program, which the company's institutional investors were clamoring for.

By giving preferential treatment to R&D as a required area of excellence, his strategy has started to produce results. Although the company's revenues decreased from over $5 billion to $3.5 billion last year, its return on equity increased from 16 to 24 percent and its stock has rebounded to $60.

Another CEO who understands the concept of giving areas of excellence preferential treatment is Ken Derr of Chevron. Since the price of oil plummeted in the 1990s, most oil companies have been reducing their exploration budgets significantly. Exxon did so by 12 percent, BP Amoco by 22 percent, and Conoco by 40 percent. Kerr did the opposite. Recognizing that reserves are what increase the value of an oil company, starting in 1989 he boosted the exploration budget higher and higher as a percentage of revenues. The result: Chevron has increased its reserves to 4.3 billion barrels, a 165 percent replacement rate compared with an industry average of 116 percent.

Areas of Excellence Are Nurtured over Time

Many companies whose strategy has been successful over a long period of time have nurtured their areas of excellence over long periods of time as well. Pioneer, the Iowa corn seed king, dominates its rivals because it has deliberately cultivated the skill of gene juggling to a higher level than any competitor.

The company literally "pioneered" the development of hybrid seed corn. The company develops more than 20,000 hybrids per year, of which only a few dozen make it to market. And it has been doing this for 70 years. Since 1926, starting with its founder, Henry A. Wallace, the company has given preferential treatment to research—as a technology-driven company should. In Pioneer's case, it's called agricultural research and the company spends more in this area than any of its competitors. Pioneer has more biochemists and molecular geneticists working in state-of-the-art laboratories than any of its competitors. In the last three years alone, the company has invested over $1 billion in research, a sum far greater than its competitors' budgets combined. And this investment pays off for both Pioneer and its customers.

In the last few years, Pioneer has introduced over 100 new hybrids that account for over 40 percent of the company's revenues. Its customers benefit as well, and this is where Pioneer's competitive edge is seen in the marketplace. Farmers judge the performance of hybrids on the basis of yield, or the number of bushels per acre. Pioneer hybrids produce an average of 5.8 bushels more yield per acre over their closest competitor. The advantage widens with every extra dollar the company invests into research—its *area of excellence.*

Importance of Areas of Excellence

Why are areas of excellence an integral part of strategic thinking? No company has the resources to excel as a competitor across all these areas of skill. Therefore, another strategic decision that management must make, once the driving force has been decided upon, is to clearly identify those two or three skills that are critical and to give those areas *preferential* treatment. In good times, these areas receive additional resources; in bad times, they are the last areas to be trimmed.

Knowing what strategic area drives your organization together with the corresponding areas of excellence that are required to support that strategy is akin to understanding what *strategic weapon* will give your organization a *distinct* and *sustainable advantage* against your competitors. Understanding the concepts of driving force and areas of excellence makes life for the CEO and the management team much easier as they decide which products, customers, and markets the company should, and should not, pursue and thereby allocate resources more effectively.

Pulte Corporation
PULTE

Making the Rules
in a Chaotic Industry

Robert Burgess
Chief Executive Officer

Changing the rules in an industry that has no established rules isn't easy. First you have to *create* them. And that, in many ways, is what Pulte has done in the U.S. home building market. The industry as a whole has very little structure and few established business models. The result is a generally chaotic, opportunistic market. A few years ago CEO Bob Burgess and the management of Pulte Corporation decided to set themselves apart from every segment of the marketplace, establishing a new model—a national home builder with consistent quality, a coherent national structure, and sophisticated marketing as its foundations.

"Our competition is everybody from a handful of national home builders to regional or local building companies to the guy in a pickup truck," says Burgess. "The industry as a whole has not generally been very good at marketing, at producing consistent quality, at branding—all the things successful consumer companies do. So we've tried to change the rules by building those skills to a degree that some regional builders, but no other national builder, has been able to do."

And it's paid off in exceptional growth. But to understand how the company got to that point let's go back to 1994. Burgess had been in charge at Pulte for a couple of years, coming from a diverse corporate background—notably, a stint at GE under Jack Welch. He came to believe that the direction of Pulte was somewhat vague and confusing to both man-

115

agement and the investment community. "We were operating a number of unrelated businesses with over 70 percent of our profits derived from businesses that were in some way related to home building but were not really our core business," he says. "Although we were one of the largest builders, I don't believe Wall Street or our employees truly understood what direction we were trying to achieve."

In order to bring needed focus to the business and improve the efficiency of its operations, Pulte's senior executives decided to use DPI's strategic thinking process. Through the rationale of the process Pulte's management team agreed that the future lay in its ability to establish and build upon the company's core home building strengths. "We brought our corporate and field management teams together to candidly assess our strengths and areas of competitive advantage," recalls Burgess. "We wanted the best input and complete buy-in from our entire senior management team."

The strategic thinking process enabled all levels of management to develop a common understanding of this new future direction. The team's consensus was that Pulte had strayed from its core business, wandering into several loosely related businesses in which it could not be a leader. "One thing I learned from Jack Welch," says Burgess, "is that if you can't be number one, two, or three, you should not be in that business." Consequently, the new strategy called for a clear emphasis on home building and a goal of becoming the best production home builder nationally and even internationally.

Burgess credits the DPI process with enabling his team to formulate coherent goals and a direction for Pulte, adding: "It channeled our discussion toward a single focus for the company. While we started out considering a multitude of approaches and ideas, we ended up very strongly in agreement."

Burgess cautions, however, that "the initial session of the strategic thinking process is only the tip of the iceberg. The real benefit of going through the process is what your people do about it in the weeks and months that follow. It has caused us to raise the level of our strategic thinking both in the field and at the corporate office."

Plan 2000

On the basis of the outputs of the strategic thinking process, a new long-term business plan was developed, called Plan 2000. This plan defined the company's operational, organizational, and financial goals for the next five years. After deciding on the company's strategic direction, management evaluated all existing businesses under the Pulte umbrella to determine their compatibility with the corporate direction. "It was obvious that many of our financial services operations and the building supply business did not fit our new strategic profile," says Burgess. Management then implemented a plan to divest these nonconforming businesses in an orderly fashion.

The underlying purpose of Plan 2000 was to ensure a leadership position for Pulte in all aspects of the home building business. "At a critical step in our strategic discussions," says Burgess, "DPI confronted us with the realization that an *industry leader* is a company that is able to *change, control, or substantially influence the rules of play* in the sandbox in which it chooses to compete. Pulte's Plan 2000 is designed to change many of the traditional rules of the home building marketplace."

Management then set about getting its house in order and building the Pulte of the future. The vision was to create a company that would excel, among other skills, at quality and marketing—givens in many industries, but not consistently practiced in the home building industry.

An early challenge was to bring consistent quality across all of Pulte's markets, something that has never been done on that scale in the industry. "One of the things we realized that would allow us to break away from the pack and be a real business was quality—getting it ingrained in the business. So we went out and hired a fellow who had a background with Motorola and he ran our quality processes for a number of years. He did a terrific job," Burgess states.

In addition to the physical quality of its structures, Pulte strives to interject quality into the entire experience of buying and owning a home. This includes the unthinkable—delivering and closing on homes when the company says it will. The initiative must be working, since J. D. Power, which recently began tracking the home building industry, has given Pulte consistently high marks for quality.

The next critical need was to implement better information systems. At the time, Pulte was fragmented into more than 40 markets spotted around the country; new information technology would help create consistency and the ability to share knowledge across the company. Appropriate expertise was brought in, and today new information systems are helping provide the glue that holds the structure together.

"The third building block we established was marketing," Burgess recalls, "which, as I said, was not well understood in the home building industry. Basically the rule has been to say 'OK, I've found some land and built something on it, now who's going to buy it?' Then you went on to merchandise it to a particular market or group. So we decided to *change the rules again*. We went out and got some experts in consumer marketing from consumer products companies and the automobile industry. They led us to a marketing concept we call TCGs, or targeted consumer groups, and we've actually segmented all our markets into those groups, and plan our business around meeting the needs of each group.

"For example, TCG 1 might be the entry-level, first-time buyer with no children. TCG 2 might be an entry-level buyer who has a family. Another

TCG might be empty nesters and another, retirees. We are now very involved in market research to understand the needs of these consumer segments. We then define the location and the home that will attract and keep those consumers as long-term Pulte customers. TCGs are a little different in each market, but that's what's driving our business now. Rather than reacting to a land broker bringing us a 'great' piece of land, we are now looking for specific land to target at a specific TCG customer. For example, in Atlanta we're building homes targeted at people who want to live in specific infill locations that reduce their commute time. In many instances, new homes haven't been built in these areas for many years but they are perfectly positioned for these buyer groups. Homes of this type are normally much further outside the employment corridors, where the land is less expensive. Once we locate these opportunities, we have a tremendous competitive advantage."

Homeowner for Life

All these pieces of the Pulte strategy—exceptional quality, targeted marketing, building for the needs of specific groups of consumers—have begun to generate a high level of loyalty to the Pulte "brand." And it all started with the realization during the strategic thinking process that Pulte's product—the Pulte home—would be the central focus of the future. This has enabled Pulte to develop a marketing strategy, revolutionary in its industry, that mimics a concept pioneered by General Motors—moving up with consumers as they progress through life—in a concept called the "Pulte Homeowner for Life."

Presently Pulte has developed 41 selected markets across the country in which it plans to build a range of homes suited to specific sets of TCGs. As Burgess explains, "We've taken each of those 41 markets and given ourselves the capability to have a breadth of product across each market. That means we're not just a high-end builder; we're not a low-end builder. We'll build for a wide range of TCGs in each market. We're now building our business on the Homeowner for Life theme. That means we'll serve our home buyers through the various stages of life. It's never been done in this industry before and it's a very exciting concept."

As Pulte begins to build this base of brand-loyal consumers, it has once again *changed the rules*. "We spent a significant amount of time and money attracting buyers and building the Pulte brand through targeted advertising. Branding in this business has been done well by some local or regional builders, but never on this scale," Burgess says. "And most builders drop the communication after the sale."

But Pulte has recognized the possibility to bond with satisfied customers and continues to reinforce their brand loyalty through ongoing communication. "We're communicating with our buyers all the time after they're in the house. If they've bought a starter home, we let them know about move-up homes. If they've bought a move-up in Michigan, we let them know about second homes or retirement communities in Florida or Arizona."

The concept is taking hold and becoming a reality, although, by definition, it is a long-term strategy. "We know it's working because, for example, in Phoenix 20 to 30 percent of the buyers are coming in and saying, 'We've been living in a Pulte home in Chicago or Michigan or wherever, and we're looking for a Pulte home out here.' "

To further illustrate the plan's success, Burgess relates a recent occurrence: "One day I was walking a subdivision in Florida and I talked to a woman who had bought a Pulte home in Michigan. Her daughter had also bought a Pulte home. She was telling me how happy she was and the things we had done for her. So I asked her if she had considered a Pulte home here in Florida. And she looked at me, a little amazed I guess, and said of course she was buying a Pulte home. She just hadn't decided which one yet.

"Another lady called me one day and she was mad as hell. I thought. 'Uh-oh, what did we do wrong?' But she was upset because she was in St. Louis and couldn't find a Pulte home. I said, 'Gee, I'm sorry, we're just not in St. Louis.' But that's the kind of loyalty we're looking for. And it's a completely new concept in this business."

Building on three components—brand marketing, exceptional quality, and information systems—Pulte has created a formula for sustained future growth. "These three skills really weren't resident in our industry," says Burgess. "We began a number of years ago to bring new people and talent into the company, and into the industry. We're starting to see other companies do that as well, but we've got a head start. With all those pieces in place we've had compounded 15 percent annual growth or more over the last six or seven years. And while we were doing this, growing to 41 markets, we achieved some geographic diversity. We're now doing business internationally, too. We're in Mexico and Puerto Rico and now we're looking at South America."

In a business vulnerable to economic downturns, there's always the temptation to diversify and offer a wider range of products to the target consumer—in effect, changing the driving force of the firm from product to customer class.

"Some of our competitors have gone into security systems, pest control, things like that," says Burgess. "But the strategic thinking process gave us a strategic filter and it keeps us focused on what we can be a leader in—home building. Again, if you can't control or influence the rules, don't be in that business. So we have alliances with the leaders in certain markets where we have a financial interest in their sales to our customers, but we don't have to be in and manage their business.

"We have a very lean management team for a $3 billion company and we can't afford to spend time on opportunities that don't clearly meet our strategic objectives. We could easily wander into many vertically integrated businesses that may be seductive but don't serve our core direction. With the strategic template from the DPI process we are now able to eliminate almost immediately those opportunities which don't fit, or find an appropriate way to deal with them."

The results of Pulte's strategic shift speak for themselves. "There's no doubt that we are now much more focused on long-term growth in shareholder value," Burgess says. "The entire organization is directing its attention to what it will take to reach the goal line we set out for ourselves in Plan 2000." Pulte is clearly becoming the home building industry leader and is playing the innovator's role in the way the housing "game" will be played in the future.

8

The Concept of Strategic Leverage

"We're a highly decentralized company with several autonomous business units, each with different products and different customers in different markets against different competitors. Therefore, the strategic thinking process should be applied at the business unit level—because, after all, it is business units that compete, not companies."

I am certain that this is a statement that you have heard before, since it has been the prevalent school of thought since the 1970s. Again, DPI represents the exact opposite school. In our view, it is *companies that compete and* not *business units.* We have come to this conclusion by observing our most successful clients, those that succeed over *long periods of time.* Their success is due to the fact that they have mastered a very simple formula: *They have learned to leverage their driving force and areas of excellence across the widest array of products, customers, and markets.*

Honda is a good example of a company that practices this formula (Figure 8-1). What is Honda's driving force? In order to answer that question, we need to look at the scope of Honda's products—cars, motorcycles, lawn mowers, chain saws, and more. What is common across all of Honda's products? The answer: engines. "Engines for the world" was Mr. Honda's stated strategy. Honda is only in the car business because cars require engines. If someone ever invented a car that did not require an engine, Honda would move on to something else very quickly.

In 1998 Honda announced the development of an internal combustion engine that emits *no* pollutants, thus meeting the year 2000 California emission standards. The company also announced that it would introduce the new engine in the 1999 Accord. How long do you think it will take

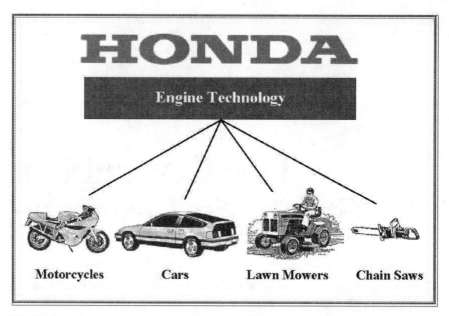

Figure 8-1. Leveraging engine technology at Honda.

Honda to insert that new engine into all its other products? The answer: 12½ seconds! This is how Honda will *leverage* its driving force, engine technology, into all its products in order to make each business unit more competitive against its respective competitors.

This is called *strategic leveraging.* Strategic leveraging says: Change the equation that states that $1 + 1 = 2$ into one that says $1 + 1 = 3$, $1 + 1 = 4$, $1 + 1 = 5$, and so on. If all the decisions that management makes affect only *one* product, *one* customer, or *one* market at a time, in terms of growth, the organization is running in place. Any company can make those types of decisions. To accelerate growth and outpace competitors, management must learn to *leverage its decisions across a multiplicity of products, a multiplicity of customers, and a multiplicity of markets—simultaneously!*

Canon is another company that is into a wide array of products and markets, everything from photolithography machines to cameras to copiers (Figure 8-2). Canon is in these businesses because each business unit draws on the driving force of the company, which is *optics.* Looking at a company in this manner can also explain its periodic failures. In the late 1980s, Canon made a massive push to enter the PC business. After all, this was a very seductive opportunity. Growth was running at a rate of 30 to 40 percent per year and Canon also knew a lot about assembling hardware. Massive push, massive failure! Why? Have you ever seen a PC with a lens? No lens, zero probability of success. It's as simple as that. That PC did not draw on the driving force of the company. On the other hand, if Canon ever figures out how to put a lens into a PC in order to make the PC do things that other PCs cannot—like scanning—then Canon may have a winner.

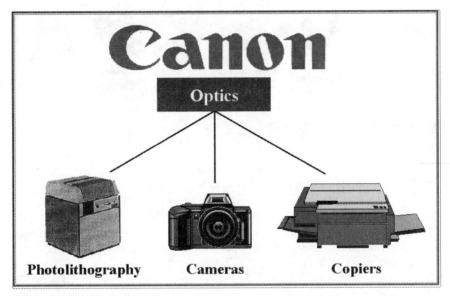

Figure 8-2. Leveraging optics at Canon.

Sharp is into an even wider array of products and markets—everything from calculators to instrument panels for airplanes (Figure 8-3). The company has dozens of business units all with different products and competitors. The business units look very different from each other. The common thread, however, is that they all draw on the driving force of Sharp which is *optoelectronic technology*. In other words, liquid crystal displays (LCDs).

Sharp has a family tree of over 200 products, all of which stem from LCDs (Figure 8-4). Sharp is a company that practices the concept of strategic leveraging to the nth degree.

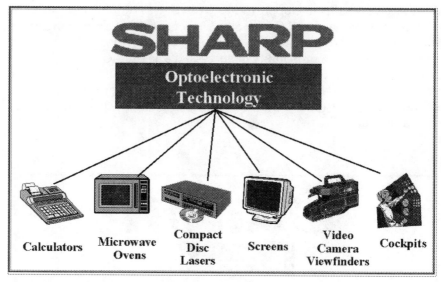

Figure 8-3. Leveraging optoelectronics at Sharp.

In this part of the world Nortel is into a broad array of telecommunication products and markets, all of which stem from the company's "digital switch software" (Figure 8-5). As noted in Nortel's strategy statement, whenever the company does something to improve its knowledge of digital switch software, it looks to "spread across as many products, customers, and markets as possible," as quickly as possible.

3M is still another company that understands this concept. All of 3M's 50,000 products stem from its knowledge of polymer chemistry and its application to adhesives and abrasives (Figure 8-6). 3M has, like many companies, periodically strayed from its driving force and gotten into other businesses, either by design or by accident. Each time it did so, 3M found itself in unfamiliar terrain and eventually abandoned those businesses.

The master of strategic leveraging is Michael Eisner, CEO of Disney. In only a dozen years, Eisner has grown Disney from $300 million to over $25 billion, an annual compounded growth rate of over 25 percent. His formula is very simple. Each year, Eisner invents a new character such as Aladdin, Ariel, or Mulan and creates an animated film around that character. Before you know it, that character appears as a life-size entertainer at Disneyland and Disney World. It then shows up as a doll in all Disney retail stores. It next appears on video format at all Blockbuster stores. It is then seen on TNT cable television. It then appears on millions of T-shirts

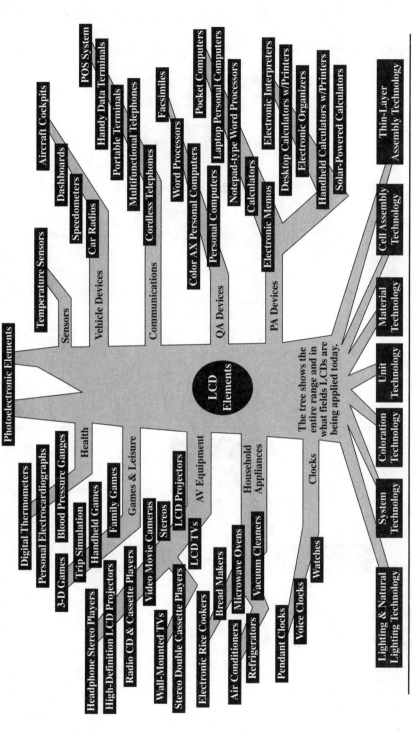

SHARP'S EXPANDING WORLD OF LIQUID CRYSTAL DISPLAYS (LCDs)

Figure 8-4. The Sharp family tree.

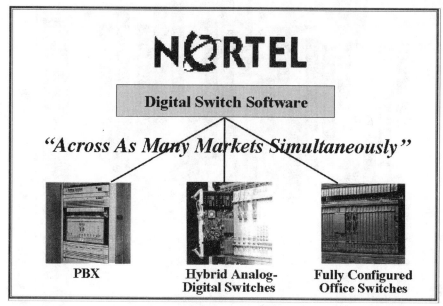

Figure 8-5. Leveraging digital switch software at Nortel.

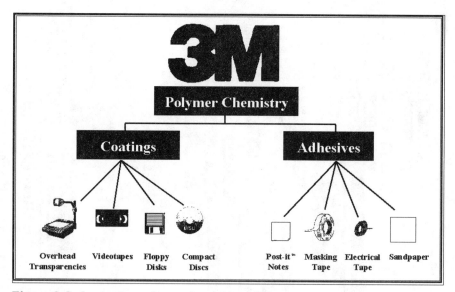

Figure 8-6. Leveraging polymer chemistry at 3M.

and coloring books. And so on and so on. *One decision leveraged across a multiplicity of products, customers, and markets simultaneously* is what allows a company to grow faster than its competitors.

Which brings us to another myth—that as a company gets larger, its growth can be expected to decelerate. When I was with J&J in the early 1960s, the company was experiencing double-digit growth. Thirty years later, J&J is still growing at those rates with no indication of a slowdown in sight.

Size is never an impediment to growth. Lack of strategic leveraging, on the other hand, becomes a major impediment to growth superior to that of your competitors. Strategic leveraging across products and markets imbeds you more deeply with customers and makes them more reluctant to leave for another competitor, thus locking the competition out.

Groupe Cantrex, Inc.

CANTREX

Reversing the Business Concept

Claude Lalonde
President

We've all seen it happen. In towns and cities everywhere, trusted independent retailers are closing their doors—victims of what the industry calls "power retailers" and "category killers." Huge chains like Home Depot, Best Buy, and Future Shop move in with massive purchasing clout, pervasive market presence, high brand-name recognition, and sophisticated marketing.

This was the environment in which Cantrex, a Montreal-based buying group for independent retailers, found itself in 1994. The company began in the 1960s when a group of independent merchants formed a co-op to take advantage of volume purchasing. The group was eventually incorporated as Cantrex in 1982, and it grew and prospered. By the 1990s, Cantrex was purchasing products for 1300 stores in the furniture, floor covering, appliance, electronics, and photography sectors. But the crush of the large-surface stores and power retailers was taking its toll. In 1994 sales were at about $460 million and *falling*.

"I believe the company had reached maturity in terms of the life cycle of its business concept," says Cantrex president Claude Lalonde. "Cantrex was mainly a buying group offering some marketing services. But we felt that providing members with volume rebates and elementary marketing services was not enough to allow them to compete in the marketplace. We had to provide them with more sophisticated marketing support. There was an increase in large-surface stores and power retailers. Our members were pushed out of primary areas, and had to compete in secondary and tertiary areas because of the influence of the category killers. Sales for 1994–1995 were decreasing and we felt we had to change our approach."

Cantrex management decided to recruit some assistance to create a new strategy to reverse the business's decline. "The name DPI came up with very good references," says Lalonde. "We knew some people who had used DPI's strategic thinking process and were very happy with the results. We were looking for a firm to help us with a strategy creation process. What attracted us—and scared us a little—was the way it is done, with managers working on the strategy as a group. We were a bit skeptical that we could come to a consensus with 30 managers participating. It's difficult enough to get consensus with five or six people around a table. We also thought that our situation was different, that strategic thinking might not work for us. But our references said no, it will work. So we went ahead. I must admit that 30 managers sitting around a table to develop a strategy was pretty scary at first. But we did come to a consensus and we're very pleased with the result."

Reflecting on the first three-day session of the process facilitated by DPI partners Mike Robert and Jacques Gauvin, Lalonde recalls the turning point where the new direction began to fall into place. "At the point where we were trying to decide on our possible driving force, there was no consensus at first. That was the basic problem with our organization. We were looking for a new avenue or another way to go, but we had no common vision of what we could be. We had four teams and even though the same topics were discussed in each team, they each came up with a different driving force. One group said user/customer class, another said service concept, the third said size/growth. The fourth one said customer class *and* growth. So you see there was no consensus at that point."

The next step in the process, after selecting potential driving forces, was to "paint a picture" of what the company would look like in the future under each scenario. Through that exercise the group was able to come to the unanimous conclusion that its future driving force should be user/customer class. The implications for the company were monumental and represented a 180-degree turnaround from its former concept. What had been a purchasing group would now become a marketer of a much broader range of services to its user/customer class—the member retailers. This meant providing, in addition to purchasing capabilities, such services as market research, marketing programs, new retail concepts, merchandising concepts, and financial services. New skills, people, and systems would be required, and Lalonde and his managers realized that it would take time to develop the new capabilities.

Says Lalonde, "The major change that we made in our business concept, when we said we would be customer class driven, is that we now provide, directly or indirectly, all the services our retailers need to succeed in a profitable way. We're being transformed from a buying group to a retail marketing group in terms of being involved with our members at the consumer level. We came to realize that very often the independents don't have the resources or the time to fully analyze the marketplace, and we had been depending solely on their input to understand their markets. We felt it was our responsibility to switch and become a retail marketing group—not only giving them more volume rebates, but helping them increase sales and reduce the cost of operations. It totally changed the direction of our company."

180-Degree Turnaround Strategy Emerges

"This was a revolution," Lalonde says of the major transition that was about to take place in Cantrex's business. "We had a management meeting after we went through the process, and everyone was in agreement on our direction. We were just beginning to make progress on the critical issues, and we didn't want to become overwhelmed by the task before us. So we used visual examples to describe how we would succeed. We said we had to cross a river and everybody could see the other side of the river, but we didn't want to try to jump all the way to the other side. It was not possible and we would fail. But there were rocks in the river and what we *could* do is jump on the first rock. Then we would see other rocks and eventually cross the river. So we said to our people, 'Move, leave the shore,' so that we could start to go in the right direction."

As a starting point, the company was restructured to accommodate the new direction. It was concluded that as a buying group, Cantrex had relied on central billing and negotiation of volume rebates as its core competencies. But as a retail marketing group, Cantrex could no longer be a single unit because each market—furniture, electronics, and the others—required specialized knowledge and skills. To that end, four divisions were established. By the second half of 1995, things began to move in the right direction.

"People were starting to innovate," says Lalonde. "We made two alliances, one in electronics and one in floor covering, which had a very positive impact in the following years. At the beginning of 1996 we made our first move in electrical appliances, buying Corbeil, a specialist in that sector. Our intention was to be a dominant specialist in appliances in primary demographic areas. We had only a few members in primary areas and it was tough to compete with the large-surface stores. So we decided to change the rules of play in that market. We became a dominant specialist with an integrated formula where we do the warehousing, deliver to the customer, do the accounting for all the stores, and have a central computer system, all under one name. We're now feeling the impact. It's an amazing change of direction."

The same concept—to develop dominant specialists—has been applied in different areas since then. Market research in the floor covering area, for example, led to the development of a new prototype concept store called Discoverings. It provides consumers with an extensive range of products in a more attractive environment than is typical of conventional flooring stores. The first 10,000-square-foot store was opened outside Ottawa in August 1997. The response by consumers was so favorable that merchant members of the floor covering division mandated that Cantrex design a store prototype tailored to "tertiary zones"—those with populations of less than 50,000. Two more Discoverings stores were opened in tertiary zones in 1998. The concept is expected to expand into more zones.

In the furniture, household appliance, and electronics sectors, Cantrex has formed a new retail sales concept called Furniture Trends. This plan unites merchants who dominate one of those sectors into a well-structured network. Merging several independent outlets under one banner, they benefit from a wider range of products, prices comparable to those of larger-surface stores, personalized service, and regional or national name recognition. The first store opened in New Brunswick and a second in Quebec in 1997, with more to come. Cantrex also recently acquired G.A. Finance, which strengthens its electronics sector and adds 125 merchants and $45 million in sales.

Cantrex's new concepts are continuing to evolve, and the company continues to adapt its capabilities as its businesses change. Lalonde is optimistic about the future, yet he recognizes that the organization must be allowed to develop gradually, as it moves from rock to rock across the river.

"The change was so great—no one in our industry had done anything like this before—that we have had to write the book as we go along. But we can do it because all the managers across Canada know where we are going. All our suppliers, all our dealers, know where we are going. And the results are there. It's not like the computer industry, where you can have a sudden explosion of profit. It's a long-term approach where each and every year, block by block, we'll build it and create our network. We have to create the culture and the environment and we have to prove things step by step.

"If we had not gone through the DPI process," Lalonde states, "I believe that we would be managing a decreasing business, because the independent as such is losing ground. We definitely have to form our members into dominant networks. Whether they are specialists or generalists, they have to be dominant in what they're doing."

Most of Cantrex's new ventures are in their early stages, yet financial results to date have been spectacular. At the close of the 1997 fiscal year, Groupe Cantrex's sales increased to $534.7 million, up from $457.4 million in 1996—an increase of $130 million, or 31 percent in two years. Cantrex stock rose in value by more than 50 percent in 1997, and earnings per share rose 20 percent. Gradually but surely a new model for independent retailers is taking shape across Canada. More strong financial results appear to be on the way as the new Cantrex concepts take root and grow. But that's not all. The stunning turnaround at Cantrex had an even more surprising result.

Postscript: Transamerica Likes Strategy, Purchases Majority Interest

As Cantrex's new concepts began to produce these impressive gains, others began to notice—especially the people at Transamerica Canada, the Canadian subsidiary of the San Francisco-based insurance and finance giant. Transamerica's Canadian unit had been a supplier of inventory financing, its primary service, to Cantrex for several years, and was facing similar problems—falling margins and a limited set of service offerings. To make a long story a bit shorter, Transamerica liked Cantrex's strategy so much that it purchased the majority of Cantrex's stock in a friendly takeover. Plans are to take the company private in the next few years.

Lalonde explains: "As with most businesses these days, Transamerica's margins were decreasing and people realized they only had one service for their customers. They wanted to expand their range of services, add value to those services, and create more of a mutually beneficial interdependency with customers. They had a choice: either start their own group to accomplish those ends or purchase an existing group. They saw our new strategy and realized that we were already doing what they wanted to do. They saw the kinds of changes we were going through and the results we've been able to achieve, so we seemed like a natural fit."

Cantrex and Transamerica are in some of the same markets—such as furniture, electronics, and electrical appliances—where synergies may be possible. Cantrex also is involved in other markets not shared by Transamerica—notably, floor covering and photographic supplies. Likewise, Transamerica's markets include products not shared by Cantrex.

"What they would like to do is to apply the same type of strategy we're pursuing to their different markets—motorcycles, recreational vehicles, marine products, and so on. They're working with independent dealers as we are, so in their minds, the strategic approach can be the same. Eventually, we will be integrated into Transamerica, but that won't take place until we're taken private."

Meanwhile Lalonde and his team continue to press on, making significant progress. "Peter Kelly, president of Transamerica Canada, told us that we are further along in some businesses than they had originally thought, particularly at Corbeil, the only franchise we have in Cantrex. For us, it's a research and development center for the type of services we provide. As we develop expertise in new services at Corbeil, we can offer them to our other dealers," says Lalonde.

If all goes according to plan, these kinds of innovations in retailing can be reproduced in appropriate businesses across the newly combined companies, building a stronger company overall. "Transamerica has seen the difference between our results before and after going through the DPI process and how our business has turned around since changing our strategy. If you look at graphs of volume and profitability, the change is drastically upward," Lalonde states. "The plan is to use the same strategy to produce the same kinds of changes and results in their business."

9

Managing Your Competitor's Strategy to Your Advantage

In spite of all the literature written about competitive techniques and competitive tactics, there are two instances in business when all these tactics and techniques are completely irrelevant. In other words, competitors don't matter.

The first situation is when you have a monopoly. The second is when there is plenty of growth in a market to satisfy everybody's appetite. In both cases, who cares about competition? A good example of the second phenomenon is the personal computer industry. During the past ten years or so, how much time did Compaq spend worrying about Dell or Dell about Compaq? A lot or a little? You're right! Very little. Why? Because the markets are growing at the rate of 30 to 40 percent per year and that is more than enough growth to satisfy everyone's appetite. However, as the rate of growth slows down in the next ten years, how much time do you think these companies will spend looking at each other? You're right again! A lot more.

Therefore, there is a very large "preamble" to the guidelines I am about to enunciate to help you manage your competitor's strategy to your advantage. The preamble is this: You and your management team have set an aggressive goal of growth for the business—and, so have your competitors. You have looked around your industry and have concluded that there is not enough growth to satisfy everyone's appetite. Therefore, your growth must come at some competitor's expense. This has to be a conscious decision by management for the following guidelines to apply. However, if this decision has been made, then the guidelines are the following.

Control or Influence the Sandbox

A successful strategy allows you to *control,* or at least *influence,* the sandbox your have deliberately chosen to play in. What do I mean by control? An example: Which company has been in absolute control of the worldwide computer sandbox for the last 40 years? Has it been Unisys? Or DEC? Or Honeywell-Bull? Or Wang? Or ICL? Of course not. The company that has been in total control on the hardware side has been IBM. Which companies have done things recently to *influence* the rules of play to their favor? The answer, naturally, is Intel, Dell, Sun, and Compaq. Microsoft, on the other hand, is in total control of the software sandbox. Companies that have been trying to influence this sandbox to their favor include Netscape, Oracle, and Linux. The jury is still out as to whether they will succeed.

> LESSON 1: If your strategy does not control, or at least influence, the rules of play in your sandbox, that is a clear signal that your strategy is not working and it is time for a rethink.

Choose Your Competitors

If you wake up each morning with a severe pain in the middle of your back and, when you look into a mirror, you see a great big competitive arrow there, that's a clear signal that you have a reactive, defensive strategy while your competitor has a proactive, offensive one. In other words, if every day you are surprised by yet another competitive tactic, this is a clear sign that your strategy is not working. It's time for a rethink.

> LESSON 2: A successful strategy allows you to choose your competitors rather than have your competitors choose you.

Predict Your Competitors' Behavior

Although many so-called competitor experts will tell you that competitor behavior is not predictable, I come from the exact opposite school. Competitor behavior is *totally* predictable once you understand a few simple things about the competition. And I happen to be in good company. Consider this self-revelation from an industry leader:

> We are a very predictable company. What we did with Windows on the desktop, we're doing with Windows NT on the server. What we did with Office on the desktop, we're doing with Back Office on the server.

The author, obviously, is Bill Gates of Microsoft. The interesting element of this statement, however, is that none of Microsoft's competitors have figured it out. If they had, they would have been able to compete with Microsoft in the marketplace rather than in the law courts using the Justice Department as their Trojan horse.

Another example can be found in the disposable diaper business. If you ever wander to that section of your supermarket, you'll find two major brands—Huggies and Pampers. Huggies come from Kimberly Clark while Pampers come from Procter & Gamble. So here are two companies slugging it out with a similar product, offered to similar customers, at similar prices. Each company, however, is there for a radically *different* reason and would behave in a totally different, but totally *predictable* manner given the same circumstance.

Thus, the first thing to understand in order to predict a competitor's behavior is that competitor's driving force (Figure 9-1). In other words, what is *driving* that competitor to that product for that customer in that market? Kimberly Clark's driving force is production capacity. It so happens that diapers need cellulose for absorbency, and it's the only reason Kimberly Clark is in that business. It's simply another place to utilize X percentage of its mill capacity. P&G, however, is there for a radically different reason. Its driving force, since its origin, has been user class—namely,

COMPETITIVE BEHAVIOR IS *PREDICTABLE*

**Mill Capacity:
Cellulose Production**

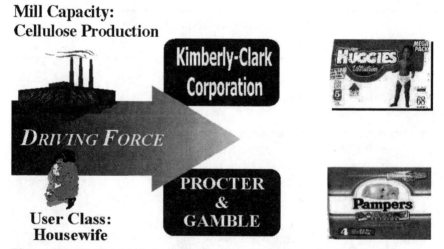

Figure 9-1. Predictable behavior in the disposable diaper business.

the female household consumer. It so happens that this consumer periodically needs diapers, and it's the only reason P&G is in that business.

Let us suppose that Dupont, the chemical giant, were to invent a new synthetic fiber 20 times more absorbent than cellulose. Let us try to *predict* each competitor's behavior in view of that event. First, what do you think P&G would do about this new synthetic material? You are right! P&G would buy it immediately. It would sell off its paper mills and convert to synthetic mills in a flash. The reason is simple: user class—the female consumer—is the heartbeat of its strategy and P&G will abandon its paper mills long before it abandons this user class.

How would Kimberly Clark respond? Probably by trying to improve the absorbency of its own product, which would not likely be a factor large enough to close the gap. The company then might reduce the price somewhat, but that still would not reverse the trend. Eventually, it might exit the market and look to utilize its capacity somewhere else. Kimberly Clark is not married to user class, as P&G is.

Predictable Behavior in the Automobile Industry

To predict a competitor's behavior, then, you need to understand three things about that competitor. First, you need to understand that competitor's *driving force*. Second, you need to understand the *business concept* that the competitor is practicing around that driving force. Third, you need to understand which *areas of excellence* the competitor is more proficient at than anyone else. Once these three elements are understood, you can predict the future behavior of any competitor. The automobile industry provides good examples (Figure 9-2).

Mercedes' concept of the "best-engineered car" is a good example of a *product-driven strategy*. The product is a car. However, Mercedes has its own concept of that product—namely, a car that is the "best-engineered." As a result, the product has a certain "look," the customer has a certain "look," the price has a certain "look," and the company goes down a certain road.

Then along comes Volkswagen. It also is pursuing a product-driven strategy. However, its concept of its product is different from that of Mercedes: "Volks" or "people's car." As a result, the product has a different look, the customer has a different look, and the price has a different look. Volkswagen and Mercedes go down different roads and the two never intersect.

And then along comes Volvo—also pursuing a product-driven strategy—but with a slightly different product concept than either Mercedes or

Competitive Behavior
Is *Predictable*

STRATEGIC HEARTBEAT DRIVING FORCE	COMPANY	BUSINESS CONCEPT
PRODUCT	(Mercedes-Benz)	"Best Engineered Car"
PRODUCT	(Volkswagen)	"People's Car"
PRODUCT	VOLVO	"Safe and Durable Car"
PRODUCT	BMW	"The Ultimate Driving Machine"
PRODUCT	GM	"A Car For Each Income Strata"
TECHNOLOGY	(Honda)	"Engines For The World"
TECHNOLOGY	SAAB	"The Intelligent Cars" (Avionics)

Figure 9-2. Predictable behavior among leading car manufacturers.

Volkswagen. Volvo's concept, since its very beginning, has been the "safe and durable car" with the accent most likely on "safe." Again, the product has yet a different look, the customer has yet a different look and so has the price. Volvo heads down a third road that doesn't intersect with the other two.

And then along comes BMW—another product-driven company—but with a slightly different concept of its product. "The ultimate driving machine" is what BMW keeps telling us. The emphasis on "performance" leads BMW down a fourth road.

Finally, along comes General Motors. What is GM's concept of its product? Sometimes, to uncover a competitor's strategy, you need to go back into that company's history. In the case of GM, you need to go back to the mid-1920s, when Alfred Sloan was chief executive. His strategy, enunciated in his 1972 book *My Years with General Motors,* was very succinct: "a car for each income strata." In other words, as Americans moved up into higher income levels, they had another GM car available to buy—from a Chevrolet to a Pontiac to a Buick to an Oldsmobile to a Cadillac. The second part of Sloan's concept was just as succinct. It stated: "as such, GM cars must look distinguishable one from the other."

In other words, if GM is to ask its customers to pay higher and higher prices as they migrate up through the brand chain, then each model should have a few bells and whistles that are different enough to justify that higher price.

Which brings us to another circumstance that causes the strategy of a company to change by accident rather than by design. That circumstance is when management *loses sight of the very strategy that has been at the root of its success for a long period of time.* That has been the case with GM since the early 1970s. GM, as we all know, was attacked by the Japanese car manufacturers during the 1950s and 1960s. By the early 1970s, GM was reeling from that assault. After losing large chunks of its markets, GM management took a quick trip to Japan to explore what advantage the Japanese had. Quick trip, quick conclusion: "Cheap labor—$1500 per car cost advantage. Therefore, we must reduce our costs. Therefore, we must streamline our manufacturing process. Therefore, we must make all our cars fit the same manufacturing system. Therefore, what do we do with the design?" Simple. Make all the cars look alike. When GM went down the "look-alike" road, GM management lost sight of the very strategy that had been at the root of its success for 70 years.

Proof of this thesis is Ford. Ford's strategy, since World War II, was simple: "copycat GM." In other words, whatever model GM introduced, Ford had a similar one a couple of years later. Until 1970. When Ford saw GM go down the look-alike road, Ford finally said to itself: "Not this time." And guess who started making "distinguishable-looking cars"? Ford, naturally. Fiesta, Escort, Taurus, Sable, Navigator. In fact, Ford to this day is practicing GM's strategy—by default—because GM management gave it up. Which company has had more success against those same Japanese competitors? Ford, by some $20 billion. In the early 1990s, even Chrysler noticed what was going on and it too started making "distinguishable-looking cars" with so much success that it attracted Daimler Benz's attention and was soon gobbled up.

The Fallacy of Critical Success Factors

There is a school of management that has been preaching for many years: "In any one industry, the rules are the same for everyone. Therefore, there are two or three generic critical success factors at work and whoever masters these, wins the game." After 20 years of working with over 300 companies across many industries and in dozens of countries, I have never found that to be true—even once. Instead, what I have discovered is that in one industry, several competitors can be in the same sandbox because they have the same driving force. However, they are usually practicing slightly different business concepts so that, under the same circumstance, each will behave in a slightly different manner.

Honda is also in the car business. But what is Honda's driving force? As described in a previous chapter, Honda is a a company driven by technology—specifically, *engine technology.* In the 1970s the EPA imposed emission standards on the car manufacturers. What did the top five companies mentioned above add to their product to meet those new standards? The answer: a catalytic converter. Not Honda. Honda went back to the root of its strategy—the engine—and changed the technology in a manner to meet the standards without the need for a catalytic converter.

Now for *predictable behavior.* In light of Honda's strategy, what other, different products might we expect Honda to entertain in the future? Locomotive engines, then marine engines, and eventually aircraft engines? Not a bad progression. Look out GE, Rolls Royce, and Pratt & Whitney. In fact, if I were running one of these three companies, I would have had an antenna dug deep into Honda's R&D program, since Honda could turn out to be a worse competitive nightmare for me than the ones I get from my two current competitors. Guess what? The nightmare has arrived. After 14 years of me offering this up as a possibility (check my two previous books), Honda did introduce a new *aircraft* engine in 1998 (Figure 9-3).

Figure 9-3. Predictable news at Honda: the turbofan aircraft engine.

Saab is also in the car business. What is Saab's concept of its product? The answer can be found by looking at what other business Saab cars stem from. In other words, what was Saab's original business? The answer: jet fighters. As a result, Saab's strategy is to make "intelligent cars" through the transfer of jet aircraft avionics. If you attack Saab, it will react in yet a different, but totally predictable, manner. Saab will put fins on the side of the car, a turbo engine in the back, and a cockpit in the front seat. That's Saab's roots. That's what Saab will always revert to in order to defend itself.

LESSON 3: A competitor's future behavior is totally predictable once you understand that competitor's driving force, business concept, and areas of excellence.

The Vince Lombardi School of Management

Whenever we sit down with a DPI client to discuss the possibility of growing at the expense of a competitor, the client's immediate reaction is to analyze the competitor's strengths and weaknesses, zero in on the competitor's biggest weakness, and attack it. This is the prevalent school of management today and it is one that gives us, at DPI, great difficulty.

The reason is simple. If you attack a competitor's weakness, what will the competitor do? Correct it, naturally. You now have converted that competitor's weakness into a strength. Now you need to attack a second weakness. What will the competitor do again? Correct it. You have given the competitor another strength. The logical, but somewhat absurd, ending to this scenario is that you will make that competitor so strong that it will put you out of business!

A good example is found in the 15-year war between AT&T and MCI, now part of Worldcom. After suffering losses of millions of customers to MCI, AT&T decided to strike back. In mid-1999, it introduced a special product for corporate customers that bundles together a range of different services all at the same discounted rate whether the call is transmitted over wire or wireless. This product's objective is to take advantage of MCI Worldcom's lack of wireless capability, seen as a major weakness. What does MCI do? It enters into talks to buy Nextel, a wireless provider, and turn that weakness into a strength very quickly.

Attacking a competitor's weaknesses is not strategically sound. What to do instead? You must go to the very essence of the competitor's strategy and *choke it off*. I call this the Vince Lombardi School of Management. When Lombardi put his offensive team on the field, where did the first five plays go? In his book, he explained his strategy very clearly. Before each game, Lombardi would identify the four best players on the defense and that's where the first five plays were directed. His concept was very simple. If his team broke through the best part of the opponent's defense in the first five minutes of the game, game over!

If you attack a competitor's weakness, the game gets played between the 40-yard lines. Up five yards, back ten yards. No one gets to the end zone to score in a big way. In business, if you attack a competitor's weakness, *no significant shifts in market share occur.* Significant shifts occur only if you go at the essence of that competitor's strategy and attack there.

Two companies lobbied harder than any others to incite the Justice Department to initiate an antitrust suit against Microsoft. Which two companies were these? Oracle and Sun Microsystems. Why did they orchestrate this effort? Simply because Microsoft had introduced products that were aimed at the very essence of each of these two companies' strengths—Sun servers and Oracle relational databases, respectively—and Microsoft was winning. If anything, Microsoft was sued for outthinking these two competitors. If Sun and Oracle had read this book, they would have been able to "read" Microsoft's strategy, anticipate the attack, and been ready to defend themselves in the marketplace rather than cry foul to the Justice Department lawyers.

> LESSON 4: Significant shifts in market share occur only by attacking the root of a competitor's strategy.

Two Choices: Imitate or Obliterate?

Once a client is convinced of the futility of attacking a competitor's weakness, the natural tendency is to say: "Let's, instead, identify the competitor's driving force, business concept, and areas of excellence and then try to outperform our competitor in those areas. My view is that now you are getting into a marathon with no finish line. A excels. B outexcels. A passes B. B passes A. Get the picture? No one gets to the finish line. What you are doing in this mode is aping or cloning a strategy by trying to outperform a competitor in the capabilities it is best at. As noted in Chapter 1, you do not grow at a competitor's expense by *imitating* that competitor's strategy. Why? Because the competitor has invented the rules and understands them much better than you. The competitor has an organization structure in place to police and enforce those rules and probably has more money than you. Therefore, the competitor can outlast you at the table. Remember, the odds range from 1:1 to 1:0 in favor of the house. You eventually will lose!

What should you do instead? You need to *neutralize* a competitor's strategy by *changing the rules of play*. Many companies that have done so successfully were mentioned in Chapter 2. Why does this approach work? When you find a way to change the rules of play, you place your competitors in a position of having to reconsider how they conduct their business. In order to implement their strategy, they have put into place an organization structure, processes and systems, skills and competencies, and compensation programs to do business *one* way. When you change the rules, they have to rethink all these aspects of their business and, frequently, cannot bring themselves to make any changes. While they are agonizing over "what to do," they are paralyzed and *not* playing the game. In fact, they are on the sidelines and while they are there, you can make significant inroads at their expense. You have, in fact, effectively *neutralized* your competitors' strategy!

LESSON 5: Significant shifts in market share occur only by neutralizing a competitor's strategy by changing the rules of play in the sandbox.

We mentioned in Chapter 1 how Xerox saw its market share dwindle from 97 percent to 12 percent as a result of Canon's ability to enter the market by changing the rules of play to its favor—specifically, by selling the copiers outright rather than leasing them and by going through distributors instead of a direct sales force. It took Xerox five years to wean itself from its leasing revenue stream, and it took the firm seven years to make the decision to sell through dealers—85 market-share points later.

The most effective tactic you can devise to neutralize a competitor's strategy is to turn a competitor's *unique strength* into a *unique weakness* in one stroke. This is what Canon did to Xerox. What had been one of Xerox's unique strengths—the cashflow stream from leasing—became a unique weakness in an *instant,* when Canon started selling copiers outright.

Dell did the same to IBM and Compaq. By selling direct and eliminating the middleman—the distributor—Dell turned the extensive, multilevel distribution system, which had been a unique strength of these two companies, into a unique weakness.

Craig McCaw of Cellular One accomplished a similar feat against AT&T. By using a wireless technology, he turned AT&T's unique strength—the most extensive copper wire network in the world at the time—into a unique weakness. This tactic paralyzed AT&T for ten years. Not until Mike Armstrong became CEO in 1998 was AT&T able to craft together a coherent strategy to respond.

A more contemporary saga is the one that is unfolding at Merrill Lynch. Cofounder Charles Merrill served as CEO from 1940 to 1956 and gave the firm its strategy of bringing "Wall Street to Main Street." To execute that strategy, the company built up an army of 18,000 retail brokers located in 1000 offices in 45 countries. The company prospered very nicely for several decades until Charles Schwab arrived on the scene in the 1970s and completely changed the rules by offering stock trades at considerable discounts—$39 versus $400 for an equivalent transaction. Two decades later, Schwab had an even greater impact on Merrill Lynch when it changed the rules again by being the first to transact trades online over the Internet. This initiative completely paralyzed Merrill Lynch, because people who trade online do not require a broker and Merrill has 18,000 of them! Overnight Merrill's unique strength became a unique weakness. If Merrill goes online, as it has announced it will do, it will have a mutiny on its hands in the form of thousands of brokers who have already expressed their opposition to trading online. If the company does not go online, it may miss one of the most important changes in selling methods to come along in a century and, as a result, may not survive as a financial institution.

The current CEO, David Komansky, agonized over this change in the rules of play for *four years* before coming to his recent decision online. In the meantime, Schwab has increased its customer base by 1.5 million in the last two years, has seen an increase in profits of 29 percent compared with Merrill's decrease of 35 percent, and enjoys a market cap that exceeds Merrill's by $2 billion.

As the theme of this book has been throughout, companies who win in a major way have a strategy that sets them apart from their competitors by changing the rules of play to their favor.

OM Group

The Importance of Strategic Focus

Jim Mooney
Chief Executive Officer

It's probably the greatest war game in the world," says Jim Mooney, president and CEO of OM Group. "You create a vision, develop a stronger army, bring on new weapons, bring on new growth. You don't let any of your people get hurt and it's all nonviolent. How much more fun can you have?"

Recent history is filled with companies that have tried, as OMG has, to grow with mergers and acquisitions as a key component. Many would agree that, in the end, it's really not much fun. AT&T and RJR Nabisco come to mind. These companies failed to follow a principle that has been the guiding light at OMG. Have a clear, distinctive strategy, a differentiating set of strategic capabilities, and build on those—and *only* those.

By keeping a strategic focus, OMG has grown from $2 million in 1971 to nearly $500 million in 1997, with productivity and profitability that far outpace the averages among its peers in the chemical industry.

The story began in 1946 when Mooney Chemicals was founded as a small family-owned producer of metal-based carboxylates—specialties used in the tire, paint, and petrochemical industries, among others. When Jim Mooney's father retired in 1979, Jim became CEO. He is one of 14 brothers and sisters, and in the early 1990s his stockholder siblings decided to cash out and sell their equity. It was up to Jim and Mooney Chemicals' management to come up with a way to satisfy the family's wishes—and set the company on a new plan to grow.

Fortuitously, one of its suppliers, Outukumpu, a Finnish mining concern, was planning to exit its business in cobalt, one of Mooney's critical raw materials. Jim Mooney saw in this the opportunity to provide a way out for the Finnish company, enhance Mooney Chemicals' business, *and* raise enough cash to buy out the family's interests as well as Outukumpu's. A deal was hammered out to merge Outukumpu's Kokkola cobalt salts business, Vasset, a small French carboxylate company, and Mooney to form OM Group. The plan called for OMG to go public, raising enough capital to buy out Outukumpu's and the family's interests.

Building a Uniform Identity

The elements of future success were clearly there: a strategic integration of a low-cost material supply, supported by international production, product development, and marketing. Yet some imposing obstacles to success remained to be resolved.

Despite complementary skills and capabilities, the companies appeared to be operating on different driving forces. More daunting was the fact that the companies had been operating in different economic systems. So some fundamental strategic, operational, and cultural conflicts needed work. At the suggestion of one of Kokkola's directors, Mooney decided to use DPI's strategic thinking process to help the management team work through the difficult issues it faced. In the course of the initial three-day sessions, several conclusions emerged.

"We thought we had two driving forces," says Mooney, "and we did. There were also the conflicting cultures of a Finnish, a French, and an American company trying to do business together as one cohesive company.

"The Finnish operation, being part of a large mining operation, was clearly production capacity driven. And the people had always worked under a government-driven system. Mooney, on the other hand, had always been product driven. It had 220 products, sold into 17 different industries. And the Americans were capitalist. So we had to come to some understanding about how we would put these companies together in a way that made sense to all of us.

"For one thing," Mooney recalls, "the top 20 individuals in the new company all came to have the same understanding of where we would take the enterprise. And it wasn't top-down or bottom-up driven. It was a consensus where the associates worked together in teams to see what we could do together, identify critical issues that would have to be resolved, and decide how we would work them out."

This consensus building approach enabled the companies to look less at their differences and more at the mutual capabilities they now commanded. Although cultural differences aren't likely to disappear entirely, they are much less of an issue today because an understanding has been reached as to the future direction of the company and the role each unit now plays in molding its future successes.

The concept behind the merger had been to combine the vertically integrated metal refining production strengths of Kokkola with the value-driven product expertise at Mooney and Vasset, and forge them into a single synergistic unit.

"We came to the conclusion that if we could take advantage of Kokkola's manufacturing capabilities and Mooney's marketing capabilities in metal-based specialties, we could make more products and provide greater geographic coverage. With this synergy we could be very successful," says Mooney. "We wouldn't be producing products just to fill capacity; we'd be creating new high-quality, value-added products that would fulfill customer needs. Ultimately, our specialized production expertise and flexibility would lead us to be a production *capability*-driven company.

"Today we see ourselves as transforming metals into specialty chemicals. Before, the Kokkola unit saw itself as refiners of cobalt and nickel metals and Mooney as a producer of metal-based specialty chemicals." The difference is subtle, but it remains the key to OMG's strategy.

Four years and a major acquisition later, Mooney would say that the creation of this common strategic understanding "brings a unique culture to the organization. It's not an American culture, or a Finnish culture. It's not a Taiwanese or Congolese culture, but is an OMG culture. No matter what nationality they are, the people understand it. They understand the vision of the company, that we are results-oriented people. They understand the successes. They want to buy into and want to be part of the successes. And that extends to the customer, and the supplier, and the shareowner. That carves out something that has lasting power."

But of course success didn't happen overnight. Before any of this would be possible another hurdle had to be cleared—the IPO, which was issued in October 1993. And largely because OMG had a well-thought-out plan, the stock opened at $8.50 and by 1997 had increased in share value more than threefold.

The successful IPO enabled OMG to follow through with its plan to buy out Outukumpu's interest in the firm and allowed the family to realize its equity.

How Vision Attracts Investment

"We've been well received by the markets for two reasons," Mooney continues. "The first is our performance, which has been very good. The second is that we've been able to communicate our business in a way that the market can understand. Without the strategic thinking process helping us, that story would not have been as clear.

"For the first time we had a uniform identity for the company. Because of this, the Finnish owners were more comfortable that we were capable of bringing it to the marketplace. And it made the investment bankers more comfortable, because they really understood our key drivers for growth and earnings.

"The easiest way to describe our business is with the concepts developed through the strategic thinking process," says Mooney. "The best thing about it is you don't have to give away your secrets, but you do let them know how you think. They know that they're buying a metal-based specialty chemical company with growth opportunities. It's real simple, that's what we are. We're nothing more than that. We're not going to look at anything else. They know that we have a global presence. They know that we have ongoing new product development, that we have an advanced and proprietary production capability. They know that we have long-term reliable supply relationships that feed that production capability. They know they're buying into a company with experienced management that understands the external environment as well as the internal environment. They understand how we focus on niche markets and what areas we want to go into, what areas we don't want to go into, based on our strategic focus and discipline. They know where we want to expand our existing product range. They know where targets are for new product development, and that strategic acquisitions have to fit the criteria that we just developed in front of them. The investors can see we have absolute discipline in our focus, and that there is no variation from that.

"We're getting ready to do a public issue," Mooney explains. "And if I didn't have the concepts developed through strategic thinking, I don't know how I would explain this thing. The first thing they always tell us about our business is it's too complicated. You go to 30 markets and you have 250 products. You have global capabilities. You're buying material out of Congo and Zambia, which are politically unstable. And they can give you a million reasons why they can't buy our stock. But once we go through the operational strategy that we use to run our business, show them our vision strategy without giving away the secrets, address some critical issues, that simplifies the business real quick. Growth through metal-based specialty chemicals, period, nothing more than that. Niche markets, new product development, global expansion, acquisitions—it's pretty clear what we're going to do. They don't want a public relations firm telling them what OMG is doing; they want to hear it direct."

In Jim Mooney's view, too many companies suffer from a *lack* of vision or a distinctive strategy. This hurts their chances of growing *and* convincing potential investors and customers that they will grow. Relying on "spin doctors" to position the company's story is no substitute, he feels.

"I'll go to presentations and someone will be talking about how important their investor relations or public relations department is. And I'm sitting there thinking, 'My God, if you've got to talk about that, you've forgotten what you're in business for. You don't really have a vision. You're trying to create a vision where there isn't one.' Investors will support you with a clear vision. They won't support you if all you've got is a public relations manager. People see right through that. I can't tell you how many companies I see that have good operations people, but they have no vision as to where the company's going, what's driving it. They'll actually say, 'Well, you know, we had a bad quarter last one, we may have a bad quarter this one, but we're doing everything we can. We're going to fix it.' I'm sitting there thinking, 'Holy cow, how can you even go to work like that?'

"And you see good companies, good fundamental technologies, good fundamental production capabilities, good fundamental marketing skills, and they can't deliver a vision that will bring shareowner satisfaction, that will bring customer satisfaction. Even if you've got all those fundamentals going for you, if investors and customers don't *understand* your vision, they'll have trouble going along with you."

After the IPO: Acquiring to the Driving Force

Since the beginning, OMG has pursued a plan to grow in three areas: acquisitions, new products, and geographic reach. Guided by strategic filters, clearly agreed upon by the entire management team, OM Group appears to be succeeding in making the plan work. This built-in compass helps OMG target only opportunities that leverage production capability.

"When our people develop products or look at markets or identify acquisitions, they know exactly where we're headed, they know what we're looking for," says Mooney. "They know when they see an acquisition and they bring it to my attention whether this fits in, whether it's metal-based specialty chemicals, whether it's something we can leverage with our production. We don't want to get into a 'me-too' application. We look for new product potential, whether it offers new niches, whether it fortifies the current weaknesses we have or builds on strengths. These are the critical issues we have to look at.

"That's the great thing about it. Based on our production capability, if we've identified a new product, we identify where the customer will use our product. We understand what the size of the potential growth is, we understand what the product return is, the profit, and we go after selected markets on a geographical basis. Everything is based on leveraging our production capability technology and the raw material resources within the product."

OMG's most recent acquisition is a good example of this line of thinking. And by initiating the new venture with the strategic thinking process, OMG quickly recognized synergies and opportunities to leverage its driving force.

"We just made a substantial acquisition. We bought a company called SCM Metals, which expands our metal-based powder business into copper. Now we can leverage both the copper and the cobalt from a refining standpoint and pick up new niche markets where we can find new opportunities. We went in there and said, 'Wow, they're in metal powders, so are we. They use smelting technology, we have smelting technology. They go into about 15 different markets, so do we. Their raw material costs are in copper. Lo and behold, over half of the cobalt that we refine has copper in it.' We came in from a very different standpoint than they did. But together, we realized, we could take that copper on a low raw material cost basis, utilize our production capability, and take advantage of it. And our stainless steel powders have a lot of nickel in them. OMG has a vertical integration in nickel. So these are opportunities. And we talked about the particle size of the powders. OMG has tremendous particle size technology. With SCM and OMG combined, we've even *enhanced* our technology, which is driven by our production capability, and we know how to make it happen. See how they fit in?"

As he builds OM Group, Mooney is adamant that the company will grow as a cohesive unit, interlocked by its driving force—its specialized production capability in metal-based specialty chemicals—and vision. To say it, though, is one thing. To do it, another. So the CEO goes into each acquisition using the same approach that has been successful for OMG to date.

"The first item on my agenda in running the business is to look at the operational objectives and understand them," he says. "The second order of business is to put people through the strategic thinking process. The pure reason I do this is so that everybody understands where the company is headed. It builds trust, it builds confidence, it builds opportunities, it addresses weaknesses in a very positive way. This process has the unique capability of enabling you to look at your own plan and have bullets going through you and you don't feel bad about it.

"A good example is when we sat down with the strategic thinking process with SCM. There was an area of strength, or rather we realized there was a *weakness* that could be *developed* into an area of strength. Now, SCM operated with this weakness for years. And what we were able to do through the process was quickly identify this weakness that could be turned into a strength—so much of a strength that if we were successful at this, it would be a *unique* strength.

"They hadn't realized it was a weakness. Before, they didn't have the opportunity to see it that way. No one asked them to think differently. They were tied into thinking on a functional, quarter-to-quarter basis. Now we come in with this process and it gets them all stirred up, and all of a sudden they're saying this can be a real strength to the company. This is something that we can change. Who doesn't want to change the place where they're working, where they can take a weakness and convert it into a strength? At first they were thinking, 'How are we going to grow 15 percent a year, 20 percent a year? We never did that before.' Now they're thinking, 'Hey, we can do it. And this is all we've got to do.' "

Grasping the Big Picture

"At first people think that they understand strategy," Mooney says. "Yet they confuse operations and the vision, and what the larger critical issues are that have to be addressed, and what you have to do in your strategic profile to get where you want to be. After that's all laid out and there's disagreement on it and it's hashed out, there seems to be a point of consensus. At that point of consensus the critical issues that need to be accomplished can be addressed very easily. In a matter of days you can get a whole management group there. At the end of the strategic thinking session they understand what your driving force is, they understand what areas of excellence you have. And they understand another point, which is critical—timing. This method creates an *urgency*. And that urgency brings positive results.

"I think what happens is people identify the position the company is in and the opportunities they have. So there's a sense of urgency to accomplish these critical issues. This has certainly happened with OMG.

"And that's because they *were* the rationale. They're the ones saying, 'These are our strengths, this is what we do well, this is where we have the most opportunity, the external opportunities, the internal opportunities. What do we have to do? We have to leverage a production capability.' And they were able to come to that conclusion themselves. If I had tried to sell my position, it wouldn't have the strength as if *they* came to that conclusion. And not only that, when you get done, there's the compelling logic as to *why* you're doing what you're doing.

"I've always liked this about the strategic thinking process. It brings a sense of ownership, it brings a sense of entrepreneurship, it brings a sense of teamwork and consensus. The people become integrated in the process. That's what it comes down to. It diminishes egos. It diminishes the possibility of the company getting off into something that we shouldn't be into. There are so many checks and balances. Turf issues are forgotten. You bring down the walls on egos."

In the end, though, what really matters is results. And you don't have to look far to find them at OMG. Sales grew from $180 million in 1993 to $388 million in 1996 with estimates as high as $500 million for 1997. The stock rose from $8.50 to $37 in three years, for an increase in shareholder value of $627 million. Its "per associate" sales were around $850,000 and operating profit about $115,000—close to three times the industry average.

"It's because we let everybody get involved with the results," Mooney states. "It's pride of ownership. Entrepreneurship. New product development. Geographic growth. Right down the line. They're part of it. They see it. They live it."

10

Sandbox Competition and the Rules of War

Whenever I work with a client and I introduce the notion of warfare, someone points out: "This isn't war, it's only business." My response is the following: "It isn't military warfare, but it's commercial warfare." In fact, most of the concepts I have discussed in this book come right out of the military, because military organizations have been the longest in existence to attempt to codify their concepts and processes. The same concepts of military warfare apply to the commercial arena and have been emulated by commercial organizations all over the world. The following are some of the rules to follow to win either military wars or commercial ones.

Rule 1: Circumscribe the Sandbox

The first decision that needs to be made is "What sandbox do you want to play in?" That decision is yours and yours alone. Your strategy must clearly identify what products, customers, market segments, and geographic areas you wish, and do not wish, to compete for. And you can make that sandbox as large or as small as you want. This decision is yours and yours alone.

The computer sandbox is a prime example (Figure 10-1). IBM has chosen to play in all four corners of the computer sandbox—worldwide: from mainframes to macros to micros to PCs to laptops to notebooks for consumers as well as commercial enterprises in all geographic markets of the world. A very large sandbox. Compaq, on the other hand, made a very dif-

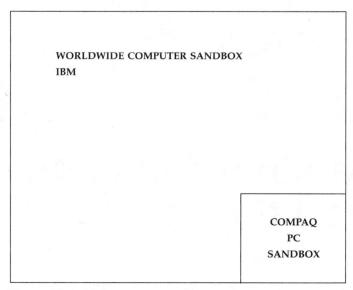

Figure 10-1. The computer sandbox.

ferent choice—at least until its purchase of DEC. Compaq began by playing in a much smaller sandbox—namely, the PC sandbox. Even there, it divided the PC sandbox into two smaller ones—the home PC and the business PC. Because it found the home PC sandbox too volatile, it decided to concentrate on the business PC sandbox. With the purchase of DEC, Compaq obviously has now decided to play in a slightly larger portion of that sandbox, which might be called the business computer sandbox.

Dell and Hewlett-Packard have made still different choices. Dell has chosen to play in both the home and business PC sandbox while HP has undergone a classic schizophrenic transformation. At its founding, HP created its own sandbox, that of instrumentation and measurement devices. Along the way, it discovered a need to get into computers and printers, both of which were required as *enablers* for its instrumentation devices. Unfortunately, the tail started wagging the dog, and the computer business became larger than the instrumentation business. HP developed a bad case of schizophrenia, which it finally resolved by dividing into two separate public entities in 1999.

Rule 2: Choose Your Competitors Before They Choose You

Which competitor do you invite into your sandbox to have a good time with? That's right. A sandbox is a place for you to have a good time, not to agonize. If your strategy is not a fun experience, it's the wrong strategy. A good strategy is fun.

The next step, then, is to examine all the competitors that are outside the sandbox looking in and determine which one at whose expense you can grow your business. You do this by identifying each competitor's driving force, business concept, and areas of excellence. Then you hone in on the one whose strategy you can *neutralize by changing the rules of play*. Against this competitor, you now construct an *offensive plan*, which you pursue with singularity of purpose.

You now must look at the remaining competitors and ask: "Who can do that to us? Who is in the position of growing at our expense, and who can neutralize our strategy by changing the rules of play on us?" Identify those companies, bring them into the sandbox, and design a *defensive plan*, which will prevent them from achieving their goal.

All too often, companies study their competitors, analyze their competitors, evaluate their competitors—study, analyze, evaluate. Then they do nothing about it! If you want to grow at a competitor's expense, you must have a plan. Growth doesn't occur by wishing it into happening.

Rule 3: Never Give an Enemy a Sanctuary

This concept comes straight from the military. Any good commander knows that if the enemy is allowed a sanctuary, the enemy will pause to hone its skills and come at you later, but stronger. In business, never allow a competitor into your sandbox without a strong response that will serve notice to your competitor that its presence is not welcomed. I call this a "shot across the bow." If the competitor doesn't retreat, then you must use your entire arsenal if necessary to escort the enemy out of your sandbox.

The best example is the Big Three automobile manufacturers in this country. For two decades, these companies provided the Japanese manufacturers an enormous sanctuary—namely, the small-car portion of the market. The Big Three thought the shabby and shoddy small cars that the Japanese first brought to the U.S. market in the mid-1950s would never appeal to the buyer of larger, more luxurious models. How wrong they were. From that sanctuary, the Japanese honed their skills by learning how to make small cars better and better. Then they invaded the "luxury" segment with the introduction of the Acura, the Lexus, and the Infiniti. The Japanese market has been growing for three decades and there is no sign of a reversal.

Another example is the war that Advanced Micro Devices (AMD) has attempted to wage against Intel with limited, if any, success. AMD entered into Intel's sandbox by offering clones of Intel's chips for the low end of the market. The rationale: since Intel seemed to be moving upmarket,

AMD could establish a "beachhead" in Intel's sandbox that Intel would not pay attention to. Unfortunately, Intel's CEO and COO proved to be better strategists than AMD expected. Intel's management quickly recognized that providing a sanctuary would give AMD the opportunity to hone its skills and establish a base from which it could then attack the remainder of Intel's more profitable, high-end business. So what did Intel do? In early 1999, it announced the introduction of two lower-priced versions of its Celeron microprocessor, aimed squarely at AMD's customers. Guess what happened? The tactic was so successful that AMD announced "it would suffer an unspecified operating loss in the next quarter due to price competition with a resurgent Intel." In fact, AMD reported substantial losses for several quarters while Intel reported a 19 percent increase in revenues and a 57 percent increase in profits for the same period.

Rule 4: Never Start Wars on Two Fronts

In other words, do not attack two competitors at the same time. We all know what happens to generals who start wars on two fronts. The last thing you want is to have two or three competitors shooting back at you. One will be enough to worry about. Target a single competitor at a time.

The Japanese, again, are masters of this concept. For example, who has Toyota had in its sight for the last 40 years? General Motors has been the target. Not Ford, not Chrysler, but GM and GM solely. Toyota's stated strategy, articulated in the 1950s, is to outsell GM in terms of total units worldwide, and eventually in the United States. Toyota in 1999 produced more cars in the United States than it did in Japan.

Who has Komatsu had in its sight for the last 30 years? Not John Deere or Case or Hitachi or Allis Chambers. The target, all these years, has been Caterpillar. The war cry at Komatsu has been "eat the Cat" not "eat the Deere."

Who has Honda had in its sight among all the other car manufacturers—not in terms of quantity of cars, but in terms of quality of cars? The target: Daimler Benz. The drumbeat at Honda has been "beat Benz, beat Benz," and Honda has done so the last three years running, according to J. D. Powers & Associates.

A more recent master of the "single target" concept is Mike Ruettgers, CEO of EMC Corporation. When Ruettgers took over in the early 1990s, the company was on the verge of bankruptcy. Ruettgers decided to bet the company on a single product. He killed nine product lines to then concentrate his entire R&D budget of $10 million on developing a super-fast storage system for large computers that would allow companies ready access to vital information. The sole target: IBM. Once the system was developed, he marshaled all his troops and focused them on IBM customers. Before IBM even noticed, EMC had taken over the market and become the dominant player. Even IBM started buying EMC's systems.

Using the same tactic in other areas, EMC has given its shareholders a 36,196 percent increase in the value of their shares in ten short years.

Rule 5: Never Start Meaningless Wars

Who has MCI had in its sight for the last ten years? The answer, naturally, is AT&T and not Sprint or GTE. Why AT&T? As Willie Sutton was said to reply when asked why he robbed banks: "That's where the money is!" AT&T is where the money is: 80 percent market share compared with Sprint's 7 percent and GTE's 2 percent. The moral: do not start wars over a 1 or 2 percent shift in market share; it's not worth the battle. If you are going to start a war, make sure there is a lot of booty to be had at the end. In other words, aim for significant shifts of 20, 30, or 40 percent in market share.

Rule 6: Never Start a War Without Weapons

A few years ago, MCI introduced a product called "Family and Friends." It was a program that allowed groups of people to call at a similar low rate. During this period, MCI took 17 million customers from AT&T. Why? When MCI launched the product, the company had developed special software to bill groups of people on networks. MCI knew that AT&T did not have such software and that it would take AT&T two to three years to develop it. Thus, MCI had a weapon to last the war.

The same is true in business. Do not start a battle without the weapons to last the war, because the laws of physics kick in whereby every action brings an opposite, and equally violent, reaction. And that leads us to our next rule.

Rule 7: Never Go to War with a One-Step Plan

Before you launch your first missile, make sure that you have anticipated the competitor's reaction, your next move, the competitor's response, and so on. There will be a chain of actions and reactions and your plan must take these into consideration if you are to succeed in growing at a competitor's expense.

Rule 8: Listen to the "Music"

An unfortunate fact about the tons of information that companies accumulate on their competitors is that most of it relates to current or *past behavior*, which has nothing to do with the competitor's future direction. Instead, you must gather relevant data—namely, information about *future intent*. General George S. Patton said it best:

> I've studied the enemy all my life. I studied, in detail, the account of every one of his battles. I've even read his philosophers and I've *listened to his music*. I know exactly how he'll behave under any set of circumstances. Unfortunately, he hasn't the slightest idea of what I'm going to do, so when the time comes, I'm going to whip the hell out of him.

In order to monitor future intent, you must listen to the *sounds, noises, and themes* that companies emit about their intentions in the future. That "music" is more important to your ability to manage a competitor's strategy to your advantage than anything that competitor has done in the past.

American Precision Industries

API

Building a Vision of the Future

Kurt Wiedenhaupt
Chief Executive Officer

"Managing companies is like standing with your management team in a valley, and you're surrounded by many beautiful, and challenging, mountain peaks. Your strategic objective here is to decide which mountain you're going to climb," says Kurt Wiedenhaupt, CEO of American Precision Industries, in discussing his approach to creating and implementing strategy.

"Now, there are various ways of doing it. The first way is to sit in an armchair as boss, point at one peak, and say 'charge.' The people are charging up and they come to the first difficult spot. They say, 'Do you think this guy is serious? Why don't we take a rest here. He's still down in the valley.' And then after a while they say, 'We're not crazy,' . . . and then, 'Forget it.' They come back to the valley and say, 'It was too difficult, it was too dangerous, and it didn't make any sense.' Then the boss gets upset and everyone wonders what comes next.

"The second way is that the boss says 'charge,' and he's in front of these guys. Then the only difference is that when they come to the difficult spot, the boss makes the decision that maybe that wasn't the right mountain to climb, so they go back into the valley and try another one, and another one, and another one. They are very busy and expend a lot of energy and money. And the reason they turn back this time is that they are not sure that it was the right peak to climb in the first place.

"There is also a third approach," says Wiedenhaupt. "Here you get conviction because you very carefully select the mountain you want to climb together, and everyone knows the reason you want to climb that mountain. Then you start working your way up together, and if you hit a rough spot, a crevasse or overhang, you will find a way around, and you will get to the top. The team will think it out because everyone is convinced and *knows* it's the right peak to climb.

"They know the logic, the logic that says to everyone it's the right thing to do. There's ownership, there's pride, there's determination. And the team is united in it. As an alternative, you have only a strategy that is developed by the boss, or by somebody from the outside. So in a team of 20 you might have two or three who are enthusiastic, then you have four or five who are followers, and the rest are leaning back."

When Kurt Wiedenhaupt came to American Precision Industries as the new CEO in 1992, he saw no lack of mountains worth climbing. The questions, of course, were which ones and how? Wiedenhaupt had such consistent success with the strategic thinking process in previous assignments as a CEO that he resolved early on to use it to identify the mountains and the means.

Separate but Equal Strengths

API is a "mini-conglomerate," a collection of three technology-driven divisions with no real strategic connection to one another. One is in precision motion control, one in industrial heat transfer, one in electronic components. Each has a unique technology at its core. But no synergy potential exists among the divisions, given widely divergent technologies, applications, and markets.

"These three have nothing to do with one another," Wiedenhaupt explains. "That's the way I inherited the company. There had been others, but these divisions were the ones that were left over when I arrived here. It was a dormant company that, at one time, had grown but was not growing anymore. There was no clear strategy for future growth. Sales had moved from $38 million to $50 million in the 12 years before—below the inflation rate. The company was profitable. There were good products and good people. But there was no R&D, no vision of the future.

"So I had to give the company a vision, a future. That was my main job, to define the future, to communicate it and get the company moving. And I knew only one effective way of doing it—the strategic thinking process.

Within the first month I took three groups separately offsite, and we developed strategies for each of them."

Kurt Wiedenhaupt is a strong believer in the ability of the process to draw out the knowledge, experience, and honest thinking of the participants, as long as the CEO doesn't try to dominate the discussion or manipulate the outcome. "I was a very attentive listener," he says. "The only thing I told the people before we started each session was that the good news is I cannot interfere in the process. I do not have a preconceived idea of where we will take this company. The only thing I know is, we're going to grow the company. But you are the ones who will decide the strategy, not I. The bad news is, whatever you decide, I will make sure you implement, so you better make the process yours, and that's what happened. The three technology groups developed strategies. Then, based on that, I developed my own thoughts with DPI's help, for the company as a whole."

This is a somewhat unusual application of the strategic thinking process, since most companies are looking for a way to coalesce the various and sundry business units together into one synergistic dynamo. "One thing I recognized immediately was that I was not running one company," Wiedenhaupt states. "I was running three companies. And it would have been wrong to push all the three groups through the same filter."

As the teams sorted out their future strategic profile, and ultimately the profile of API as a company, the key question became: By what route would profitable, stable growth be achieved? By building on each individual technology? Seeking further unrelated technologies? Looking for synergistic, interrelated technologies? As part of a technology-driven company, the teams decided to focus API's growth on the diversification of products and markets based on the three core technologies. By combining the R&D strengths of all the business units, and leveraging each unit's technological strengths, the company could begin to generate new, differentiated products. These products would provide opportunities to strengthen API's position in current markets and offer opportunities to break into selected new markets. This two-pronged expansion would then be bolstered by acquiring companies with a direct relationship to these core technologies, thus opening up new geographic and market opportunities.

On the macrostrategy level, the plan was to create new growth—when the core technologies wound down at some point along the road—by building *interrelated* technologies on the strengthened foundation of the three original business units.

"So we did it," Wiedenhaupt says, "and got the critical issues moving. The board approved the strategy in December, when I presented it officially, and we started implementation in late 1992, early 1993. The rest is really history, because we grew the company in four years from $50 million to $250 million."

An Expert's View
of the Strategic Process

As the first client of Decision Process International back in the 1980s, Kurt Wiedenhaupt has a unique perspective on the strategic thinking process. Wiedenhaupt tried out the DPI process with his management team. It was so successful in creating a cohesive strategy that he used the process several more times to help management teams sort out strategies in subsequent assignments. He had identified something new in the process and its mentor that was a refreshing change from other methods of strategy creation he had encountered.

"I have been exposed to McKinsey, Boston Consulting Group, and Bain & Co. They are all very capable and I'm sure they have a good product that's extremely impressive," Wiedenhaupt says, "and I'm sure intellectually they're also very sound. The only problem is their product is not of the people, by the people, through the people. It's not owned by the people who later have access to it. It is an alien product no matter how well it relates to the company. That's why it fails. I think, *intellectually,* they might even come up with a better product than the process we are using. But when it comes to executing it, they are miles behind DPI. It's simply ownership. We as human beings do what we *believe* in, and we do that with *enthusiasm.* If somebody else tells us something to do, we might do it, but don't expect any enthusiasm.

"Anyone who is considering using the process should not see it as a one-time exercise. It has to become part of the company, part of the everyday life. Language like critical issues, driving force, areas of excellence, strategic thinking—this is part of our daily verbiage. It is part of our language, part of our culture now. I just came back from a three-week holiday, my first in five years, during which I wrote a manual for our company. In it I describe our systematic approach to business. And I describe the strategy process so that new people who come into the company, after reading that manual, understand our philosophy, our processes, our systematic approach to business. I describe the strategies, the decision analysis, the problem analysis, the Strategic Product Innovation process, and the annual planning process so that a new person reads it and is immediately an insider. This way people start to adopt it, to live with it, and it gets stronger and stronger."

Strategy and the New CEO

Having been called upon several times in his career to take the reins of businesses he did not know as an insider, Wiedenhaupt has come to recognize that strategic thinking can be an especially valuable tool to the

CEO coming into a new situation—either as incoming chief executive or in the integration of a new acquisition.

"This process, I have found through my own experience," he says "can be beautifully used by *any* new CEO coming into a company or business he is not fully familiar with. You have the opportunity in a very short period of time to immerse yourself into this new business. You get a deep understanding of the issues. You get a very good feeling for the players in your organization who are participating in this process. And I have to say it took at least half a year out of the learning process in my last assignment. I feel much more secure in the path I'm walking because my own people have described that path and they are walking with me.

"No matter what industry you come from, what industry you go into, the fact is that when you enter a new company, you enter a different culture, a different and new business environment. The most important thing for you is to learn to listen and not to tell people what to do until you really know what you're talking about. And going right away into the strategy session and sitting there and listening helps you get to know the people, their thinking, their emotions. You get to know the issues, the real issues the company has to address. So by just going through the strategic thinking process you get tuned into the company much faster than any other way I know.

"We have just acquired a company in Germany, and we are going through the process immediately," says Wiedenhaupt. "Any company we acquired over the last four years went through the strategy process because it's so important—not that we don't know what to do with the company, but we want to make sure that the people develop their strategy, and that they see the light, and that it is their product and they take ownership."

11

The CEO as Process Leader

"Follow me," T. E. Lawrence shouted to his Arab troops as he led his army's charge into battle.

Although the term "leadership" is frequently used to describe successful CEOs, few executives in business today can be considered true leaders. The litmus test for any leader is whether he or she will be followed as Lawrence of Arabia was followed by an army of people who were not of his race or religion. For the followers to allow themselves to be led assumes their implicit belief in the leader's ability. Followers want to know where they are being led.

Many books have been written on leadership, but few have been able to describe it in comprehensible terms. Nor have they been able to describe the skills of leadership in any detail except to attribute it to a "trait of personality." John P. Kotter, in his 1988 book *The Leadership Factor,* explained that leadership can be defined, analyzed, and learned. He also pointed out that it is not taught in business schools. Unfortunately, he did not articulate in his book how leadership skills can be acquired.

Jack Welch, CEO of General Electric, views it this way in a *Business Week* interview:

> A leader is someone who can develop a vision of what he or she wants their business, their unit, to do and be. Somebody who is able to articulate to the entire unit what the unit is and gain through a sharing of the discussion—listening and talking—an acceptance of that vision. And then can relentlessly drive implementation of that vision to a successful conclusion.

The flip side of this position was summed up by Roger Smith, former CEO of General Motors, in a *Fortune* interview. In explaining his failure to turn that company around more quickly, Smith cited the "inability to communicate his vision of General Motors earlier and more frequently" than he did.

Welch's definition of leadership is probably as close to the mark as any we could conjure up ourselves. However, hidden in this definition is the assumption that the CEO has mastered the skill of *strategic thinking*, the process used by a CEO to formulate, articulate, communicate, and successfully deploy a clear, concise, and explicit strategy for the organization.

A Fundamental Skill of Leadership

Many CEOs are good strategic thinkers. The problem, however, is that they practice their skill by *osmosis* and are not conscious of its various elements and steps. As a result, they do not use the process systematically. They may also have great difficulty transmitting their ability to their subordinates. The reason is simple. Whatever cannot be described cannot be transferred.

Our experience at DPI suggests that most people who surround a CEO are not good strategic thinkers themselves. Again, the reason is simple. Managers are so engrossed in operational activity, so isolated in their functional silos, that they have not developed the ability to think strategically. A CEO, therefore, may wish to involve subordinates in a deliberate application of the strategic thinking process strictly for its educational value for both the CEO and his or her subordinates.

The Role of the Process Leader

There is only one person in any organization who can "drive" the strategic thinking process and that is the chief executive of that organization. *Strategic thinking, then, must start with the CEO.* Strategic thinking is definitively a trickle-down process and not a bubble-up one. It is a very interactive process, but the CEO must be its owner. As such, the CEO must show commitment to the process by participating in all its phases and work sessions.

Because the process is highly interactive, it is not for the faint of heart. The process invites discussion, debate, and constructive provocation. Everyone, during its various phases, has the opportunity to express his or her views, have these challenged, and then challenge those of others. As a result, the process is ideal for CEOs who encourage frank, open discussion of issues and challenges.

A CEO has two options available to get a strategy implemented. The first approach is *compliance.* Here the CEO announces what the strategy is and how he or she expects it to be implemented. The CEO then assigns different tasks to different individuals. They, in turn, implement the strategy without questioning its rationale. In a world of increasing complexity, this approach has less and less appeal to more and more CEOs.

The second, and more effective, method is *commitment*. Here key executives actively participate in developing the rationale behind the strategy and assist the CEO in crafting the strategy itself. In order to ensure widespread commitment to the strategy, most CEOs include the top two levels of management in the process.

The Role of the Process Facilitator

One role that the CEO should not attempt to play is that of *process facilitator*. One cannot have one foot in the process and one foot in the content. Attempting to guide the process while participating in the debate will give everyone the impression that the CEO is trying to manipulate the process to a predetermined conclusion. Therefore, it is wiser to have a third-party facilitator guide the process along.

A facilitator is not a *moderator*. A moderator is a person who directs traffic as best as he or she can during a meeting, but without relying on a specific process. By contrast, a facilitator is a trained professional who comes to each meeting with a structured process together with predesigned instruments that keep the discussion moving forward in a constructive manner toward a specific set of conclusions. The facilitator also keeps the process honest, balanced, and objective.

As the CEO of a Fortune 10 company said to me during one of our work sessions. "You know, Mike, you're the only one in this room who tells me to sit down and I do. No one else in this room would dare say that to me."

Tangible and Intangible Results

Different CEOs use the strategic thinking process to address a variety of challenges, and they expect different outcomes from the process.

There are two categories of outputs that stem from the DPI process. The first are the *tangible* results that the process was designed to deliver. They include:

- A clear strategy and profile for the future of the business
- A list of critical issues that become the work plan for management
- An enumeration of strategic offensive and defensive objectives

- A filter to allocate resources
- A filter to choose opportunities
- A hard-copy rationale behind the strategy, to serve as a tool for explaining the strategy to others

The second category of outputs are *intangible* results, which are frequently more valued by the CEO than the tangible ones listed above. The six cited most often by CEOs are *clarity, focus, consensus, cohesion, commitment,* and *successful deployment.*

Clarity

Although not every client changes its direction as a result of using the DPI process, all clients have said that the process brought clarity to their strategic thinking. As a group, the management team usually goes into the process with slightly different perceptions of the company's strategy or, in some instances, with a nonarticulated and somewhat fuzzy strategy. When people exit the process, however, they have a crystal-clear strategy and profile of what the company intends to become. All members of the management team now possess a single vision of the organization's future.

The strategic profile can also be used to bring clarity to other people in the organization. Many of our clients have published all or parts of the strategic profile to communicate the strategy to various interested groups—for example, in annual reports to inform shareholders of the company's direction. Others have used it as a discussion paper in internal forums with employees. Still others have used it to bring the board up to speed on the strategy of the business.

Focus

Focus is another output of the process. The strategic profile produces a better tool to allocate resources and to manage the time and efforts of others. It enables managers to direct their efforts toward activities that complement the desired direction of the company and to avoid wasted efforts on unrelated issues. In other words, it ensures that people are *doing things right on the right things.*

Consensus

The strategic thinking process is structured to bring about consensus at every step. The debates and the discussions occur in a way that agreement is achieved systematically on each key issue before the group moves on to the next one. The assignments worked on during the sessions are designed to table all the key questions about the future direction of the organization. The evaluation instruments extract everyone's best thinking and provide an opportunity for each person to present his or her views, opinions, and rationale on every important element of the business. We have found that it is not sufficient to collect a person's perceptions through survey alone. People also need a forum to elaborate and explain the rationale behind their statements.

An executive vice president in one of our client companies said of his CEO at the end of a work session: "I found out more about this man's views on our business in the last three days than in the 20 years I have worked with him." This observation is echoed by many executives who have participated in the strategic thinking process.

Because the process provides a forum to discuss issues in an orderly manner, there is seldom a dissenting voice at the end of a work session. Consensus building unquestionably contributes to a more harmonious organization.

Cohesion

"Hockey stick planning," one CEO said to us, "leads to hockey puck management." Without a clear profile of what it wants to become, the organization bounces from one questionable event to another. It zigzags its way forward and expends valuable time, money, and effort leapfrogging from one suspicious opportunity to another. When there is no clear strategy accompanied by a filter to screen opportunities, management can often be seduced by the financial aspects of an opportunity, only to discover later that there is no fit with the rest of the organization's capabilities.

The strategic profile becomes the bedrock or cornerstone of management's actions and, when used in such a manner, results in the synchronization of resources instead of dispersion or fragmentation. Less time will be wasted exploring undesired options and less effort will be expended justifying the existence of the "sunset" portions of the business. Hockey puck management will disappear.

Commitment

One result that every CEO desires is the commitment of the management team to the strategy of the business. This is a key output of the strategic thinking process. The reason is simple: people are committed because it is *their* strategy. They participated in each step of its construction. All their views were heard and their inputs considered. In such circumstances, commitment can sometimes come from surprising quarters. The president of a division of a complex multinational company, whose unit was going to receive less emphasis in the future as a result of the process, commented at the time: "I recognize the fact that we're not going to get the same resources as we have in the past, but I'm totally committed to that decision. I now understand why those funds need to be given to other parts of the business."

This is an important achievement. Every organization must discriminate among its various units when allocating resources, and it is important that the managers of the less emphasized units understand the reasons they will not be treated as they were in the past. These units still need to be managed well even though they may not be the "stars" of the future. In such instances, the strategic thinking process can be a unifying force.

"For any strategy to succeed, you need operating people to understand it, embrace it, and make it happen," says Roger Schipke, former senior vice president of General Electric. We couldn't agree more.

Deployment

"It's easy to develop a strategy, it's the implementation that's difficult." This is a statement we have heard frequently over the years. One aspect of strategy is its formulation; another is thinking through its implications. Most strategic planning systems in place today do little to encourage the formulators to think through the implications of their strategy. As a result, CEOs end up reacting to events as they are encountered, and many of their subordinates start losing faith in the validity of the strategy.

"There were so many holes in the CEO's strategy, I gave up trying to implement it," is how a senior vice president of a client organization put it. Every strategy, especially one that calls for a change of direction, has implications. A good strategic process should help management identify and *proactively* manage the implications of a strategy. These implications are then converted into a short list of *critical issues* that become the work plan for management.

Critical issues are the bridge between the current profile of the organization and the future strategic profile that management has deliberately decided to pursue (Figure 11-1). Managing the deployment of the strategy then means managing the critical issues. The ongoing resolution of these critical issues will make the future profile of the company materialize over time.

Figure 11-1. Critical issues bridge the CEO's vision.

Figure 11-2. The strategic profile is the target for all decisions.

The strategic profile becomes the target for all decisions that are made in the organization (Figure 11-2). Plans and decisions that fit inside the "frame" of the profile, or picture, are pursued while those that do not fit are not. Once the critical issues have been identified and delegated to specific individuals for management and resolution, deployment of the strategy proceeds quickly and successfully.

Quanex Corporation

Quanex

Hammering Out
a Common Vision

Vernon Oechsle
Chairman and Chief Executive Officer

The next time you open a soda can or buy a new window screen, think of this: it once may have been the aluminum siding from the house you grew up in. And the company that made this metamorphosis possible may well have been Houston-based Quanex Corporation (NYSE: NX).

"We make engineered steel bars and aluminum sheet, both processed from scrap," explains Quanex chairman and CEO Vernon Oechsle (pronounced X-lee). "It's all recycled. Our plants are called minimills in the metals industry. We're the only company that runs both steel and aluminum minimills. We also have a third business that makes what we call engineered products, and those tend to be formed products. We take some of our aluminum sheet and roll-form it to make lineals for doors and windows or screens for the wood window industry, and a lot of other products."

Quanex takes in the scrap, chops it, burns off paint and other residue, and melts it down in huge furnaces. "In aluminum," Oechsle says, "we melt the equivalent of 36 million beverage cans a day. We don't melt many cans, but we do melt a lot of old aluminum siding and scrap from stamping operations and so forth. Then there's steel, which is our flagship business. There are a lot of steel minimills in the United States, but we're unique in that business because we make what are known as engineered steel bars. We make steel in 40- to 50-ton lots, or heats, which is less than half of what other steel mills make. And each very specialized heat we make is already sold before we melt the scrap. We know where it's going and for what application. With our unique process we also have the highest operating income per ton of any steel bar mill in the industry."

The company has been enjoying strong demand for its high-quality steel, particularly from the auto industry, which has realized that smaller, lighter parts can be made with this very strong, clean steel. Demand for Quanex aluminum sheet remains excellent as a result of years of proving to users that continuous-cast recycled aluminum is just as good as the "virgin" variety.

The company has evolved from its beginnings in 1927 as a tube and pipe business. The original business eventually became an outmoded commodity producer and was sold off a few years ago, replaced by MACSTEEL®, which Quanex established in 1976, and Nichols Aluminum, which was acquired in 1989.

"We've been building these newer businesses and changing people over time. Then we acquired Piper Impact in 1996," Oechsle explains. "So really we had a fairly new mixture of businesses, or certainly new to each other. I found myself in the role of most CEOs where I'd go to New York and tell the analysts, 'Here's the vision of the company, and here's where we're going, and here's what makes these three businesses fit together.' It occurred to me and started to become a concern that I was talking about this, but no one else in the company had heard it. There was a major disconnect between what I was talking about, what my vision was, and what the people in the company were thinking and understanding.

"They were thinking about their own specific businesses, because we're a very decentralized company. We have a very small corporate office, and each business has its own sales and engineering staff. Because people were all new to each other, and saw their activities as unrelated, they simply focused on their own businesses."

It had become so apparent to Oechsle that there was little sense of a common bond between the units, and little sense of a "Quanex vision" for the whole enterprise, that he felt something had to be done. Having read about DPI's strategic thinking process, he became convinced that it was the right way to bring the businesses together under a common strategy.

"I wanted a process to help us solve all these issues," Oechsle states. "I wanted a common vision that I and everyone else in the company bought into and believed and developed, so people would have some ownership of it. And I wanted them to understand each other better, understand their commonality. Plus, one of the concerns of any business today is developing people. Talent development has become very important to us. It's one of the issues that could be helped by having these businesses work together.

"The steel guys would say, 'You can't take an aluminum guy and bring him into steel. It's soft stuff.' Likewise, the aluminum guy didn't want anything to do with the steel guy. But all our businesses are based in metallurgical science, material science. And that seems fairly obvious to me. So there is a commonality and I was anxious for them to discover that on their own.

"What I wanted to see happen was that they would be willing to share ideas and, more specifically, train and develop people together. The job market has been tight. I think it's going to stay tight. It's very, very tough to go out and hire people and bring them in at any kind of success rate. We know from the recruiting firms that for every search that's begun, there is a success rate after three years of only about 18 percent. Therefore, the odds of being able to go out and hire people, which is kind of the tradition of metals companies, and be successful, are not very great. As a result, we need to develop our own people. Clearly someone who has worked at metals-forming and manufacturing of both aluminum and steel, particularly a young engineer, is going to be a very valuable person to the company. And I really felt we were shortchanging ourselves by not cross-training. I saw that as a wonderful opportunity to develop a lot of really good material science people."

Identifying a Driving Force

The DPI process was conducted with the corporate officers, the three group presidents, division general managers, group controllers, and group sales managers—about 30 people in all.

"They were a little skeptical," Oechsle remembers, "because I said to them up front that the main objective was to define Quanex, define the company and our competitive strengths from the CEO's chair, which they had never been asked to do before. It was a whole new idea for them. We stressed from the beginning that whatever you do, you've got to be thinking about it from the CEO's perspective, and only my perspective, or we're going to reject it. So like most employee groups, they were skeptical, not knowing what to expect. They didn't know how I thought or what I expected. Of course, I was comfortable, having read Mike Robert's book, that the process was going to help us do it."

As the group moved through the process, some interesting things began to happen. During the discussion leading up to the selection of a driving force, the CEO realized that he was going to "lose" the debate.

"I thought our driving force was technology or production capacity," Oechsle recalls, "and others thought it was production capability because we do have unique processing capabilities that allow us to make customized value-added products. I realized early on that they were right and I was wrong, but I hung on because I thought that might solidify them and it would certainly strengthen their reasoning. As I challenged them harder, it made them think about it harder and gave them more conviction that it really was our unique processing capability that is our driving force and makes us successful. Eventually I lost. Everybody was delighted that I rolled over. Of course I made a big deal out of it. It was fun."

In spite of Oechsle's good-natured "defeat," he began to see some important revelations arising from the discussion. The realization about Quanex's driving force brought some crucial new conclusions from the group.

"One of the main ideas that came out was that we do have a unique processing capability," Oechsle remembers. "It isn't just volume that drives our business. MACSTEEL has been very successful over the years with value-added processes. We don't just make steel bars; we heat-treat them, do different quality testing, and more. We might turn and polish them; we might slice them. A good discussion ensued about how we need to drive not just volume, but *value-added* volume. So our people in the aluminum business started saying, 'If we sell more painted coil, we can get more cents a pound in the market, and it costs us a small portion of that to paint it. If we sell more roll-formed product, we can double the price we get for a pound of aluminum. If we sell into distributor markets, we can get a premium. Yes, it's going to take a long time because, again, distributors have a bias about continuous-cast aluminum.' But we decided to go ahead and sell it and prove that it's as good, and penetrate that new market. And again, it's more profitable. So I think we focused more on the value-added aspects of volume as opposed to just plain volume."

Oechsle has come to believe that the strategic thinking process is a powerful catalyst that enabled his people to see the real potential for far greater achievement—doubling the size of the business, for example—than they would have been able to envision otherwise. "Without this process, I don't think they would have reached this far, because by going through the process, they were motivated, and they were thinking positively. We'd been through what our strengths were, what our weaknesses were, what's going on in the environment, all that stuff. It was obvious that we're in pretty darn good shape, and there's no reason we can't capitalize on the unique production capability that we have.

"The DPI process was a unique environment for them to come into. If I had just called them in and asked, 'What can you do in five years?' I know I wouldn't have gotten anywhere near those numbers," he states emphatically.

Progress in People Development

"The other very important thing that came out of the process was the realization that the main way that we're going to get this done, not only in the next five years, but beyond, is through our people. Getting good technical people is a problem for us. We realized that we had better make progress with people development programs. The group came up with the idea that we should recruit specialists in quality, engineering, and materials. We ought to bring in five to ten of these graduates every year, come up with a training program, and send them through all three of our businesses. I thought that was a great idea, and it will pay off for all of us!"

So despite their initial skepticism, the people who run Quanex have embraced the DPI process and now use it in their operating units to create specific growth plans for each one. The approach is one they feel comfortable with primarily because they have created, and now own, the plan.

"I believe, and of course it's been proved, that these DPI people are not consultants in the traditional sense," says Oechsle. "They're facilitators. And the process is what they offer. It's a wonderful process, and it really works. I think it's so flexible that it can work with a small corporate group, or with the much broader group that we involved. It depends on what the CEO wants to do. But it's the process that matters. And I guess I was lucky that I read the book and saw that, or I probably would never have done it.

"The greatest thing happened at the end of the sessions. Part of it was that we had never been through anything like this before as a group. But part of it too, I think, was the process—my people didn't want to quit! Mark Thompson, the DPI facilitator, said, 'Okay, that's it guys.' And normally people would get up and go home, but these guys just sat there. I mean they just sat there! They really didn't want to leave! It was great!"

In addition to the recognition of common ground that Oechsle had been looking for, he began to see immediately that tangible results—and some intangibles—would come out of this new strategy quickly and for the long run.

"We've got a lot more strategic thinking in the organization than we ever had," he says. "We came out of this thing with a five-year, detailed growth strategy which says we can more than double our sales in this five-year time frame if everybody does what they said they can do. For the first time, our people were up there committing to each other, 'Here's what I can do with my business, here's what I can do with my business.' So when we added it all up, the number was just mind-boggling to everybody. Now when they do get together a couple of times a year they're saying things like, 'How are you doing on your plan?' I had a little crystal ball made up for everybody. It shows the Quanex vision, the sales number, and the EPS number—which, if we hit, will make us all money, and of course our shareholders will be very happy."

12

Making Strategic Thinking a Repeatable Practice

How do CEOs go about determining the future of the organizations they lead? During our research we asked several hundred CEOs if they had a formal process to decide *what* the organization wanted to become as distinct from a planning process to decide *how* to get there. Over 90 percent of the CEOs said that they did not have a formal process, and many even admitted that they had never noticed the difference.

When asked how they went about deciding the future of the organization, they told us that it "kind of happened informally." In other words, by osmosis. Unfortunately, anything that is not codified cannot be institutionalized. What cannot be put into hard copy, or made visible, cannot be turned into a *repeatable business practice.* An example is a chemist who just conducted a successful experiment. What is the very next thing that chemist will do? The answer: write down the formula. Why? So that the chemist can *repeat* the experiment or transfer the formula to someone else who can obtain the same result.

The same is true in business. If you want to increase the strategic IQ of your people and the total organization, you must have a deliberate, *formal process* in place so that all decisions made are decisions whose strategic rationale is documented and can be logically defended. A CEO might also use the process to raise the strategic IQ of key people—because, as noted before, most executives who spend their careers in operational silos are not good strategic thinkers.

A typical DPI strategy project lasts 12 to 14 months. We are not on site with the client for that span of time. Instead, during this time frame, we hold five work sessions with the management team, aptly named Phases I to V (Figure 12-1). There may also be a sixth session to "reverse-engineer" the process and use it on some of the client's more troublesome competitors.

STRATEGIC THINKING FLOWCHART

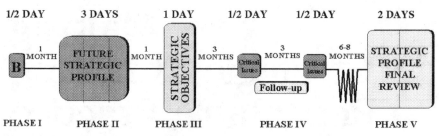

Figure 12-1. The five phases of a strategy project.

PHASE I: Briefing Session (1 half day)

This is a three-hour meeting that has two objectives:

- Provide team members with an overview of the concepts and process to gain their willing participation. Our goal is to have people go through the project voluntarily, rather than do so in order to comply with the CEO's dictum.
- Coach the management team through our Strategic Analysis Survey.

The survey requires two to three hours of work from each executive over a one- or two-week period. Our objective is to extract each person's best thinking on all aspects of the business and its environment. The survey consists of 42 questions that are designed to do an environment "scan." Completed surveys are sent to DPI for editing and collating and become the "raw material" for the next phase.

PHASE II: Strategy Formulation Work Session (3 days)

Using the combined survey responses as input, the management team comes together to formulate a strategy and to develop a future strategic profile for the organization as well as a list of critical issues that will become the "work plan" for management (Figure 12-2).

STRATEGIC THINKING PROCESS

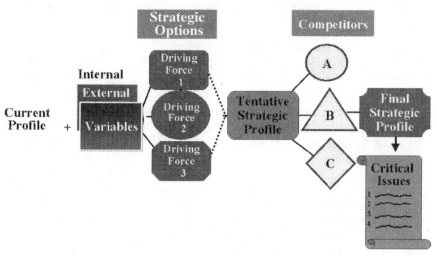

Figure 12-2. Strategic thinking provides a work plan for management.

In order to arrive at the outputs just stated, this three-day work session is divided into eight segments:

1. We work toward agreement on the current profile of the organization. The profile consists of its current scope of products, users, market segments, and geographic markets, as well as its current areas of excellence, current business concept, and current driving force. This step is an attempt at taking a "picture" of the organization in its *current* state. There can be no intelligent discussion of "what we want to be" without a clear understanding of "what we are today" and which component of the business is its current driving force.

2. The strategic variables are analyzed in order to understand the internal and external forces that will work for, or against, the organization in the *future*. This step is next in sequence because a future strategy should not necessarily be an extrapolation of the current strategy. Rather, it needs to be a strategy that accommodates the variables the business will face in the future—and these could be very different from the variables it faced in the past. The team discusses and agrees on future variables and culls the list down to the *significant few.*

3. We discuss which two or three components of the business could be potential driving forces to address these variables. No company can randomly switch from one driving force to another, but many companies have available two or three areas that could become the engine of their future strategy. DPI's methodology helps the team identify what these options are. We then take these components and develop "profiles," or scenarios, of what the organization would look like if it pursued any of these avenues.

4. The scenarios combining future variables with a potential driving force are compared so the group can arrive at a tentative conclusion. We then make a "tentative" decision on the driving force, business concept, and areas of excellence together with the products, users, and markets that will receive more emphasis and those that will receive less. This "strategic profile" translates the strategy, or business concept, into a vision of what the company intends to look like "down the road." The future strategic profile serves as a roadmap of where we want to go and becomes a test bed for everyone to use when allocating resources or choosing opportunities. In this step, management agrees to a *written* business concept or strategy statement. The initial statement should be no longer than a paragraph. Our experience shows that the probability of a strategy being implemented successfully is inversely proportionate to the length of the statement. The reason is very simple: people can't remember!

5. Competitor profiles are developed. We reverse-engineer the strategic thinking process and apply it to each competitor that will be in the "sandbox." The goal is to anticipate each competitor's strategy so that we can identify actions we can take to manage that competitor's strategy to our advantage and grow at its expense.

6. Implications of the strategy are anticipated and discussed. Often, when the strategy or direction of the organization changes, the implications of that change are not anticipated; as a result, management keeps running into these implications and is continuously reactive to them. Our view is that implications can be anticipated so that management can respond proactively—by anticipating actions to manage change—rather than being at its mercy.

7. We make modifications to our tentative strategic profile and adopt it as a final profile. The formal strategic profile contains the following elements:

- A time frame for the strategy
- A driving force for the organization
- A business concept, or strategy statement
- Areas of excellence to cultivate in support of the strategy
- The scope of products that will receive more or less emphasis
- The scope of users that will receive more or less emphasis

- The scope of market segments that will receive more or less emphasis
- The scope of geographic markets that will receive more or less emphasis
- The size/growth guidelines that will be used to judge the success of the strategy
- The return/profit guidelines that will be used to judge the success of the strategy

8. We identify *critical issues* that need to be addressed and resolved for our strategy to succeed and our future profile, or vision to materialize. The list is not usually long—six to eight in total—and each issue is assigned to a specific "owner" who is then made responsible and held accountable to get that issue successfully resolved. Our friends at 3M call this "pin-the-rose time." These are the issues that become the "work plan" for management and the "strategic plan" for the organization. They are the bridge between what we are today and what we want to be tomorrow. It is the ongoing management and resolution of these critical issues that deploy the strategy and realize the organization's vision.

PHASE III: Strategic Objectives (1 day)

What is the difference between "strategic" objectives and "operational" objectives? Most executives fumble when answering this question, which again confirms our thesis that senior executives, on the whole, are not good strategic thinkers. Nonetheless, most executives are quite competent at setting operational objectives for their people.

Each year, organizations go through a ritual of setting goals and targets for their personnel and, because of this annual "practice," they have become quite skillful at it. Each department, or function, assembles once a year to make projections of what it thinks it can achieve in the next two to three years. People start by *looking back* at what they have accomplished—the numbers— in the last two or three years. They project those numbers into the future by making adjustments for price, costs, inflation, and so on. This type of planning is planning to go forward by looking in the rear-view mirror. Such "straight ahead" thinking does nothing to change the direction, and eventual look, of the company's products, customers, or markets. It takes the organization in its current state and projects it into the future in *its current state*.

Strategic objectives are different. They don't relate to any function and, therefore, are not established by function or department. Instead, strategic objectives relate to the profile of the business—namely, its products, its customers, its market segments, and its geographic markets. The concept of strategic objectives comes from the military and can be equated to "strategic positions." Before sending the troops into battle, a military commander identifies the hills on the battlefield that must be *defended at all costs* and the new hills that must be *captured* in order to win the war. The same concept applies in business.

Every organization has product, customer, and market "hills," or positions, that must be defended at all costs while it pursues others that must be captured. Understanding which is which is a key concept of winning military or commercial wars.

Phase III is dedicated to this concept. By the end of the one-day session, management has clearly identified:

- Which product positions must be defended and which ones can be given up
- Which customer positions must be retained and which ones can be given up
- Which market positions must be protected and which ones can be abandoned
- Which new product positions must be captured by our strategy
- Which new customer positions must be captured in the future
- Which new market positions are essential to capture for our strategy to be successful

With these strategic objectives in place, management can then cascade them into operational goals and targets for the organization to ensure that everyone is rowing in the same direction and that everyone's efforts are aligned to the strategy of the business.

PHASE IV: Critical Issue Review Session (2 half days)

The CEO of one of our best clients once said to me: "You know, Mike, the most important role you guys play is that of a *strategic enforcer.*"

To a large degree, he is absolutely right. Most management teams do not have a structure, or process, to use when formulating and deploying a strategy. As a result, the formulation and the deployment happen in fits and starts, and the organization moves forward and backward in a haphazard manner.

This CEO then went on to say: "What you guys at DPI bring is a structure that we don't have the willpower to impose on ourselves, and then you move us forward from one decision to the next until we get to our final destination."

The starting point for the deployment of a strategy is to resolve the critical issues as quickly as possible. Thus Phase IV consists of two half-day sessions, three months apart, to review the progress being made, or not made, on the critical issues. During the sessions, the owner of each issue presents a formal progress report. This gives management a chance to judge whether the issue is "on track" and the opportunity to make mid-course corrections.

An interesting phenomenon we have noticed at these work sessions is that *no one comes in to report "no progress."* Because DPI is present, and because the owners know that hard questions will be asked if they report "no progress," the teams usually work their buns off between meetings in an attempt to resolve their critical issue in a more timely manner than the other groups. This is why management is often pleasantly surprised that results of the strategy materialize more quickly than anticipated.

PHASE V: Review Session (2 days)

Eight to twelve months after Phase II, most CEOs want to have a review and revisit of their strategy. During Phase II, a number of assumptions are made which then lead to decisions. In Phase V, the CEO may want to validate or invalidate certain assumptions, assess the impact of these new conclusions on the strategy of the business, and identify any new critical issues that may have been missed.

Repeatable Business Practice

Almost every one of our clients will then repeat the process, at various intervals of time and at the client's discretion. Repetition is what "institutionalizes" a process in an organization and makes it a repeatable business practice. And there is no magic bullet. As the saying goes: "Practice makes perfect!"

Mail-Well Envelope

Folding Six Companies into One

Luc Desjardins
President and Chief Executive Officer

Every CEO who has acquired another company knows that, as tough as it can be to put the deal together, the real problem is creating a cohesive unit from two, three, or more companies. Since he joined Canada's largest envelope maker in 1992, CEO Luc Desjardins has been charged with forming efficient, cohesive operations out of a mosaic of acquired companies. He first tackled Supremex and then moved on to Mail-Well, Supremex's U.S. parent company. He and the management teams at both companies have achieved startling results. Here is how they did it.

1997 was a big year at Supremex. Six acquisitions in as many years had put the paper converting company at the top of its field in Canada. Rocketing from Can $0 to Can $185 million, these combined companies represented a significant opportunity for further growth—*if* the various players could develop a strategy to effectively and quickly fold the individual units into one synergistic whole.

The story began in 1991 when Schroders & Associates, an investment banking firm, bought Supreme in Quebec and Unique in Toronto. Next, they bought Innova from Abitibi-Price. Like the other companies Schroders would acquire, these companies were in the business of "converting"—cutting, folding, and gluing paper into envelopes, courier packs, and similar products. Luc Desjardins joined in February 1992 as CEO with the mandate to blend these three together, turn red ink into black, and look for further additions to put into the mix.

The next couple of years were devoted to improving the efficiency and profitability of these operations, with substantial success. With the addition of Classic Envelope in Vancouver, the company became the dominant player in the Canadian converting business. Supremex was then sold to Mail-Well in the United States, with Desjardins continuing as CEO. The purchase of Pac National Group in 1996 added the largest single piece of the puzzle, and another turnaround challenge—PNG was losing money.

1997 was a pivotal year for CEO Luc Desjardins and Supremex, as they took on this new challenge. As Desjardins recalls, "Supremex had become quite successful and very profitable. We had just acquired Pac National Group, a $62 million company. We needed to integrate this new business quickly with the Supremex Group. The first objective was not to lose any business while we put these companies together.

"If you don't do the integration properly, keeping the right people and structuring it quite fast in the right way, you end up with a shaky operation for a while with a lot of sales at risk. One more problem we had was that the Pac National Group was not profitable. So we needed to turn it around fast, and bring it up to our standards of profitability."

To get there, Supremex needed not only a strategy but, more importantly, clean, quick implementation. So Desjardins set about looking for a methodology to get it done.

"In my years in different businesses, I have had experience with different strategic planning groups. I felt what we needed was a process that was not overly analytical. I wanted a process that would allow our people in management and leadership positions across Canada to be part of the analysis and decision making. I didn't want a plan done by a consultant. So I called DPI, because I wanted a process and a facilitator who would ask the right questions—to make people think through the issues. When I saw the DPI process I was comfortable with it and we took all our units across Canada through it," Desjardins reports.

Michel Moisan, a senior DPI partner in Montreal, facilitated the strategic thinking process at Supremex's six units. The first sessions drew on the accumulated knowledge of Supremex's bright, aggressive management teams, and concluded with consensus on a unified strategic direction. More importantly, they established a set of critical issues, each assigned to a specific senior manager, which would have to be resolved for the strategy to be successful. Follow-up sessions were geared to monitoring the progress of the critical issues, then reevaluating and fine-tuning the strategy.

Says Desjardins, "We came out of those sessions with a clear action plan as to how we would get the necessary results in plant operations, equipment, management, business unit structures, product development—all the factors we needed to address to bring us the necessary profitability in a short period of time. And we accomplished that. We not only improved the overall profitability of Supremex, but added significant profit to the Pac National Group, which was not making money before. In all, we added $7 million in profit in 1997 compared with the 1996 results."

Fast Implementation Essential

Desjardins points out that simply going through the first part of the strategy process, the formulation stage, doesn't guarantee results. Critical issues must be managed and follow-ups must be done, to ensure that the plan is on track.

"DPI's strategic thinking process gave us the opportunity to define our priorities. What makes this process different from other methods are the critical issues—prioritizing, giving responsibility, agreeing on the value of accomplishing them, and continuously following up.

"We were able to achieve fast results," he continues, "because everybody believed in the strategy and objectives. And they believed they were achievable because we had early successes. So we went on implementing our critical issues in every region. The quality of implementation continues to be one of our competitive advantages. We have this outstanding team. They are so good and so fast. The combination of strategy development and strategy deployment is what is different about DPI, and what creates success."

As the company has moved these initiatives ahead, new critical issues have been brought forward and evaluated, and progress has been made on each.

"We discovered, for example, that some of our direct customers, such as large banks, had begun outsourcing their paper products, including envelopes, to one source of supply. We identified changes such as this through the strategic thinking process and got ourselves organized to deal with them. A very senior person has been put in charge of business development for these new opportunities. We took the lead and now have professional people helping us grow that new channel proactively rather than being reactive to market changes.

"This is a very specific example of how we have evaluated our opportunities and markets. We have set priorities as to markets and customer groups we will pursue, and those we will *not* pursue. There are customer segments that are not as profitable, and markets that represent growth. We made decisions about where to put our emphasis. We have been able to extend our market share with large national accounts by making it easier for them to work with us. Today Supremex is the leader in the Canadian market. But if we don't continue to look at developing new services and markets we will not be the leader or as profitable in the future. We cannot pretend that we have reached our goals. We must always be looking ahead," he says.

"Once you have a clear strategy, it is much easier to structure the business in the proper way and develop information systems that are supportive to that strategy. Because of the change in direction, we had to acquire a new set of skills. It also became easier for us to look into the future and plan the equipment base that will support our objectives. The time and money invested in the DPI process in Canada was very fruitful, and that's why I decided to use it again when I moved to Mail-Well in the United States."

Next Challenge:
The United States

During the summer of 1998, on the heels of his group's success in Canada, Luc Desjardins was tapped for a new assignment—CEO of the U.S. envelope printing and converting division of Mail-Well, Supremex's parent. With sales of $850 million, the group comprised 34 independent business units, many of which had serious overlaps in territories, products, and customers.

"Most of these plants had been an amalgamation of a lot of acquisitions over the last four years," Desjardins explains. "They had been bought, one after another, the way our Canadian business had been built. The assignment here was similar—to get them all working together and eliminate duplication of efforts, making them more productive and efficient. So the first thing I did was to get the top 20 senior managers together to go through the strategic thinking process."

Again with the help of DPI partner Michel Moisan, the group quickly came to a realization—one that many of them were aware of, yet never had the forum to deal with—that the various plants were competing with each other, externally for customers and markets and internally for capital. "Imagine, for example, a situation where customers were being called on by several different Mail-Well units for the same products," Desjardin says.

The team also uncovered a significant amount of production duplication and underutilized capacity. The need to reorganize became obvious. So the first major initiative was to put the company into a form that could make the most of its resources and serve its customers in an efficient, unified manner. The company now consists of six geographic regions, each headed by a vice president who is also a plant general manager. The competition for customers has been reduced, and the regions can now work cooperatively to improve the overall business.

As Desjardin recalls: "The process helped me on the strategic level, but it also helped me understand my management team better. It helped us prioritize our workload, gave us a clear strategic orientation for years to come, and clarified for us how we should restructure our business.

"We've changed the structure," Desjardins continues, "from 34 individual plants that all wanted new equipment, and all competed with each other, to these six regions that work together to maximize equipment and production capability, and go to market in a more comprehensive way. It was badly needed because we were not maximizing our management talent or equipment in each plant. Now we have the top talent running each region, and we can take into account all the plants in every region when it comes to equipment and productivity. There was some unutilized capacity and we'll utilize that before we buy any new machinery.

"We expect that by reorganizing the business by region we will make the best use of the corporate base, reduce duplication of investment and market overlaps, and approach customers as one strong company, producing regionally. We also have a very big opportunity now to develop national accounts. We expect our profits for the next two years to increase to the tune of about $20 million, an improvement of almost 30 percent."

As part of the implementation component of the process, the management team agreed on seven critical issues, or "steps" as Mail-Well calls them, to ensure success. One preeminent issue is optimizing the company-wide equipment base. "So we have a total action plan for the corporation, and the results we expect to achieve," Desjardins reports. Yet the strategy will achieve its full potential only if each region is working toward those same objectives.

"We decided to implement specific activities for the resolution of the critical issues in each region, to get buy-in not just from the 20 or so people who worked on the strategy for the overall corporation, but also from the people in the individual regions. So we had the regional vice presidents bring their teams together in each region and come up with their own set of steps," says Desjardins.

This kind of collaboration was unheard of at Mail-Well only a few short months earlier, when each division was pitted against the other. "They can now say, 'If you're working on that step in your region to get that result, how are you going about it? What can I learn from you to get me there better and faster?' We can all sit and talk about these issues in the same room, all using the same language to do it.

"We began the DPI process in September 1998 at Mail-Well. The excitement now is at a very high level. We can hardly wait for the bottom line to show that this is all working well. It's nice to have a strategy," Desjardins says, "but 80 percent of the game is whether you're managing those critical issues. DPI gives you a very good follow-up system to make sure they are resolved. We are now on the move to becoming the leader that we should be in our industry."

13

Megachanges That Will Challenge Every Company's Strategy

As we work with companies, more and more people tell us that change is happening faster and faster, making it impossible to keep up, or stay ahead of the curve.

Change does *not* occur quickly. In fact, it has been documented that change, particularly technology-related change, happens slowly. Most changes that will eventually have an impact on a company or industry announce themselves well in advance of the time that their presence will be felt. If you have not been looking, however, you will always get caught by surprise. "Holy mackerel! Where did that come from?"

Some examples. Electricity was invented in the 1870s, yet it wasn't until the early 1900s that it found its first commercially viable application in the form of light bulbs. What year were robots invented? The answer: 1949. Yet here we are 50 years later barely figuring out what to do with these gadgets. How about lasers? Or fiber optics? The answer: 1954 and 1956, respectively. And again, here we are some 40 years later just barely understanding their potential applications. Even the microprocessor, the current technological rage, was invented close to 30 years ago, and we have to date only scratched the surface of its potential uses. The same is true of the PC, which is now more than 20 years old and has barely begun to affect all the nooks and crannies of society that it will eventually touch.

The reason is simple. The more dramatic the technological change, the more education is required of everyone in the chain. And that takes time. Then, applications need to be found. And that takes time. Then, experiments need to occur. And that takes time. We don't hit the bull's eye on our first attempt, which means a period of trial and error. And that takes time. In fact, history shows that a new technology takes 25 to 30 years to find a commercially viable application, and then another 50 to 75 years to infiltrate all the nooks and crannies of society.

Macrochanges Versus Microchanges

Change comes in two sizes: *micro* and *macro*. Microchanges are those that affect only a portion of society or industry. For example, the legislation that the U.S. government introduced in 1997 to deregulate the telecommunications industry affected only the companies in the industry together with their customers and suppliers. Other industries were not touched directly.

Macrochanges, or megachanges, are those that affect *every product coming from every company on this planet.* These are changes of such magnitude that they give no refuge to any organization. A number of these macrochanges have occurred, or are in the process of occurring, and many people have not noticed because they are so engrossed in microchanges. In other words, they are managing at ground zero while the winds of change are swirling at 40,000 feet. When these eventually swoop down to earth, guess who will be "caught by surprise"?

Eight Macrochanges at Work for or Against Your Strategy

There are eight macrochanges currently at work that will affect every product coming from every company in one way or another. If you "haven't been looking," you will be caught by surprise. These megachanges will have an impact on every competitive sandbox in existence. For companies that have not yet detected these changes, the new order might be fatal. For companies that have noticed the changes and are monitoring their progress, a world of opportunity and prosperity will open in finding ways to exploit them. The choice is yours.

From Push to Pull Economy

From the end of World War II in 1945 until approximately the early 1970s, the U.S. economy was in a "push" mode. A push economy is one in which there is more demand than supply, and that was the scenario for most industries during that span of time.

However, with the advent of Japanese and European car manufacturers, the automobile industry was the first to cross over, in the 1970s, into a "pull" economy. Since then, every other industry has made that journey. A pull economy is one in which there is more supply than demand. Try to think of one industry in which there is still more demand than supply today. I haven't been able to come up with any either. How about your industry? Which mode is it in?

Although this change has already occurred, many executives never saw it and have been reactive to its effects ever since, and wondering why they are in that mode. Why is this change in the "monster" category? The answer: it changes the rules of play in every sandbox in which it appears.

In a push economy, with more demand than supply, the producer is king. It's the Henry Ford model of business: "You can have any car in any color you want, as long as it's black." If not, step out of the line because the person in line behind you will gladly take it. In a pull economy, the *customer* is king because there is more supply than demand. As a result, the business model changes: If you can't give me what I want, then step out of the line because there is someone immediately behind you who will.

In a push economy, it is the producer that sets the "rules of play." It is the producer that decides what the product will be, who will have access to it, where and when it will be available, and at what price and under what conditions it is offered. In a pull economy, that no longer works. It is now the customer who determines the rules of play and all the above variables are now the prerogative of the customer and not the producer.

Many people, especially financial analysts, have been wondering for the last few years why there has not been any inflation to speak of. The answer is simple: pull economy. Having more supply than demand means that there is overcapacity in all industries and no one will dare to raise prices and risk losing the business to the "next supplier in line." The car industry, as of this writing, has excess capacity of close to 20 million cars. As long as this situation remains, the price of cars will not go up appreciably.

This is also the change that is driving consolidation among manufacturers, suppliers, distributors, and customers. The objective of these consolidations is to remove the overcapacity. If you have been wondering why business has gotten so difficult, you now have the answer. Unfortunately, the situation will not change in the near future. The economy took 15 to 20 years to go from push to pull, and it will probably take 15 to 20 years to reverse itself. Sorry!

Demographics

It is a fact that by the year 2010—ten years from now—50 percent of the U.S. population will be over 55 years of age and close to 30 percent will be over

60. This is almost the exact opposite scenario from the one we have experienced during the last three decades. It is another "monster" change that will affect every product from every company for every customer on this planet. If Caterpillar is not thinking, today, about how to have its machines operated by frail old folks like me, its business will be in jeopardy. The reason: there simply will not be enough strong, muscle-bound youngsters to maneuver all the levers necessary to make a machine perform its tasks.

During a work session with the executives of a major oil company, this shift in demographics became a topic of discussion. Someone startled the group by stating that "the company should rethink the concept of the self-service gas station." The reason: as people get older, they are less mobile and may not be able to serve themselves at this type of station. Therefore, a robot, a laser, and some electronic technology might come in handy. The new scenario: as a customer drives toward the gas pump, a laser reads the license plate, checks the driver's credit, and unlocks and opens the gas tank, a robot takes the nozzle and fills the tank, then puts the nozzle back into place, electronic technology sends the bill to the customer's bank account and the company is paid instantly. The customer leaves the station without having left the driver's seat. A pipe dream? This system is being tested in California at this very moment by BMW and Mercedes (Figure 13-1).

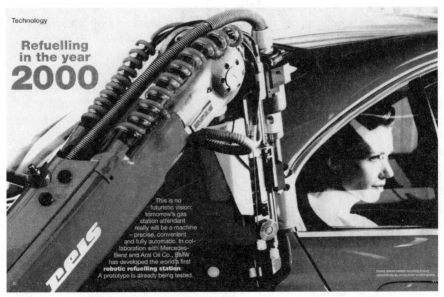

Figure 13-1. Will a robot pump your gas?

Another feature of this demographic shift already in progress is that it will trigger the biggest transfer of wealth in the history of humankind. Between $12 *trillion* and $15 *trillion* will change hands from one generation to another. This transfer will occur over the next 15 to 20 years and will have a dramatic impact on the financial services sandbox. The "transfer-ors" will need new financial products to shift their fortunes while mini-mizing taxes. The recipients will need advice on how to reinvest this windfall. Financial planners will have a field day—unless those inheriting the wealth get all the advice they need from experts who live across the country, maybe even in another country, via the Internet!

The Fall of the Berlin Wall

The dismantling of the Berlin Wall in 1989 changed the rules of play in the Western world's sandbox. The impact has yet to be felt. To date, the only consequences of that event that have preoccupied the Western world have primarily been political in nature. Politicians on both sides, East and West, are trying to install a political system to replace the bankrupt communist model. The economic model is also in transition, although it seems to be more advanced in Poland, the Czech Republic, and Hungary. Russia, the largest piece of the puzzle, still hasn't decided which model to adopt and zigzags its way forward through communism, socialism, and capitalism.

Although it may take some time for the dust to settle, the fact remains that over 300 million Eastern Europeans are slowly being brought into the "Western" economy, and that will bring both threats and opportunities to Western corporations. On the opportunity side, there is no doubt that, as their economic state improves, millions will seek out pharmaceuticals, cosmetics, designer clothes, household appliances, and other products. Great opportunities for Western companies. However, Eastern European countries have a lot of very smart people—in particular, engineers and sci-entists—and the likely result is that they will learn to be as astute business executives as their Western counterparts. Look for the entrance of many Eastern European companies into the "global" economy in the next few years. The sandbox is about to become more crowded.

The Spread of Democracy and Capitalism

Although democracy and capitalism are still on trial in Russia and many other countries of the former Soviet Union, one continent that has adopted these two models in the last ten years is South America. With Chile lead-ing the way, Brazil, Argentina, and Peru have followed suit. Again, the unfolding of events will bring opportunities and threats on a scale not seen in the last 50 years. In the next ten years, these two trends will extend themselves into Central America—in particular, Mexico. Another 300 million people will join the global "Western-type" economy.

The Modernization of China

China, like Russia, is a large communist country with a developing economy. Since the "open door" policy has been in effect, China has been edging its way toward capitalism. With the return of Hong Kong to China, that trend will accelerate. Don't be surprised if the nationalization process turns out to be a reversal, with Hong Kong's economic system becoming dominant across all of China. Furthermore, within the next ten years there is bound to be a resolution of the China-Taiwan dispute that draws these two parties closer together.

With Hong Kong's financial acumen, Taiwan's manufacturing prowess, and China's population of over 1.5 billion, an economic powerhouse is in the making. China's economy is already the fourth or fifth largest in the world, and it will be *the* largest within the next 20 to 30 years. During that time, China will breed thousands of new companies with the capabilities to make all the products that Americans want.

China will replace Japan and Europe as America's predominant competitor. That will change the rules of play for every company in the sandbox.

Digital Technology and the Internet

The growing percentage of people and organizations using digital technology and the Internet—and the increasing intensity of use—represents another change of tidal-wave proportion. The part of the business "chain" that is, and will continue to be, the most threatened and will have to learn to play to new rules is the "middleman," or intermediary. That is the case in industry after industry. The role played by intermediaries over the centuries has been twofold:

- Gatekeeper of the customer
- Guardian of the message

Historically, the intermediary claimed ownership of the customer and prevented the manufacturer access. The intermediary was also the source of information about the manufacturer's product, and thus controlled the message. All that is changing with the advent of electronics and the

Internet. The Internet allows the customer and the manufacturer to communicate directly, thus bypassing the intermediary. The shift will put pressure on all organizations that serve as intermediaries, since it will remove their "hold" on the information that they controlled and did not share with the customer.

As more and more people access this information directly, the power of decision making will shift away from the intermediary to the customer. Also, customers will have access to multiple sources for this information worldwide. At the same time, companies will be able to disseminate information about their products everywhere, regardless of geography. The open conduit will affect every product from every company on this planet.

A good example is a personal one. This past year my spouse developed a yearning for a particular Toyota car model. After visiting four car dealers in Connecticut and being told that this model was available only in California, she then went onto the Internet and obtained the e-mail addresses of six California dealers from Toyota's Web page; she sent all six dealers an e-mail with her specifications and asked for a quote. Four dealers e-mailed back a quote. She chose one, further e-mails followed, documents were faxed back and forth, and a transaction was completed *without any face-to-face meeting.* The car was then shipped to Connecticut—at our expense!

This is a warning of things to come. In the very near future, the e-mails will be directly with Toyota and not the dealer. The role of every car dealer will change dramatically in the next few years, and the dealer's "power" over the manufacturer will wane considerably. Just imagine 1000 Toyota owners getting together over the Internet and agreeing to pool their resources to place a group "buy" from Toyota, but at their price and on their terms. It is such possibilities that will give the consumer even more "buying" power.

Electronic databases and the Internet will also shift power away from the manufacturer of the product or the provider of the service to the customer. This trend will only grow, and the companies that survive will be those that have recognized this change and will be thinking of exploiting it instead of being reactive to it.

Simultaneous Convergence

One of the unique features of these eight megachanges is that they are happening all at the same time. Each one's effect on the various competitive sandboxes would be significant enough on its own; the convergence of several effects at the same time will only change the rules of play even more dramatically. Naturally, this will bring threats to some organizations but opportunities for others. Which mode will your organization be in? Will your strategy allow you to capitalize on these monster events, change the rules of play to your advantage, and ultimately control the sandbox? Or will you be caught by surprise?

Bibliography

Publications

Barron's

"Charging the 'Net" (June 1999).

Business Week

"Amazon.com: The Wild World of E-Commerce" (December 1998).
"AT&T: What Victory Means" (May 1999).
"Can Callaway Find the Green?" (January 1999).
"Can Compaq Catch Up?" (May 1999).
"High-Tech Star" (March 1999).
"How the Combination Can Pay Off" (December 1998).
"Must-See TV for Left-Handed Men Under 30" (December 1998).
"Not So Odd a Couple After All" (December 1998).
"Office Max: A Distant Third" (December 1998).
"Revving up Japan's Also-Rans" (December 1998).
"Who Says Intel's Chips Are Down?" (December 1998).

Forbes

"A Very Smart Retailer" (January 1999).
"An Edison for a New Age" (May 1999).
"Deus Ex Machina" (November 1998).
"Down on the Farm and in the Lab" (January 1999).
"Fixing an Identity Crisis" (November 1998).
"Has Corning Won Its High-Tech Bet?" (April 1999).
"Makeover at the Makeup Counter" (April 1999).
"Play It Again, Sam" (August 1987).
"Science & Savvy" (January 1999).
"Smoothing Out the Cycles" (January 1999).
"Suntel Inside" (December 1998).
"The Bull Has an Identity Crisis" (April 1999).
"The Contrarian" (April 1999).
"The Cortez of Steel Doesn't Look Back" (January 1999).
"The Push for More User-Friendly Computers" (January 1999).

Fortune

"A Dell for Every Industry" (October 1998).
"Dell Cracks China" (June 1999).

"Goldman Sachs: After the Fall" (November 1998).
"Home Depot Renovates" (November 1998).
"Larry Bossidy's New Role Model" (April 1999).
"Never Bet Against Michael Dell" (March 1999).
"Schwab Puts It All Online" (December 1998).
"Title Fight" (June 1999).

Harvard Business Review
"The Importance of Staying Flexible" (March–April 1999).

Journal of Business Strategy
"Federal Express Spreads Its Wings" (March 1986).

Time
"AT&T Betting on Its Bundle" (February 1999).

USA Today
"An Unstoppable Marketing Force" (November 1998).
"Newspapers from Home?" (January 1999).

The Wall Street Journal
"AMD to Post Operating Loss for 1st Period" (April 1999).
"Beefstakes: How Bill Foley Built a Fast-Food Empire" (December 1998).
"Intel Introduces Two New Chips for Low End" (December 1998).
"Intel Profits Leap 57%" (April 1999).
"Wall Street Is Rocked by Merrill's Online Plans" (June 1999).

Books

Ansoff, H. Igor. *The New Corporate Strategy*. New York: John Wiley & Sons, 1988.
Anthony, P. William. *Practical Strategic Planning*. Westport, CT: Quorum Books, 1986.
Avinsdh, K. Dixit, and Barry J. Nalebuff. *Thinking Strategically*. New York: W. W. Norton & Company, 1993.
Brant, C. Steven. *Strategic Planning in Emerging Companies*. Menlo Park, CA: Archipelago Publishing, 1981.
Campbell, Andrew, and Laura L. Nash. *A Sense of Mission*. New York: Addison-Wesley, 1992.
Clifford, Donald K., Jr., and Richard E. Cavanagh. *The Winning Performance*. New York: Bantam Books, 1985.
Crainer, Stuart. *The Ultimate Book of Business Gurus*. New York: AMACOM. 1998.
Davidson, Mike. *The Grand Strategist*. New York: Henry Holt, 1995.
Drucker, Peter F. *Innovation and Entrepreneurship: Practice and Principles*. New York: Harper & Row, 1985.
Georgantzas, Nicholas C., and William Acar. *Scenario-Driven Planning*. Westport, CT: Quorum Books, 1995.

Graham, John W., and Wendy C. Havlick. *Mission Statements.* New York: Garland Publishing, 1994.

Guth, William D. *Handbook of Business Strategy.* 3 vols. Boston: Warren, Gorham & Lamont, 1985, 1986, 1987.

Hamermesh, Richard. *Making Strategy Work.* New York: John Wiley & Sons, 1986.

Harvard Business Review. *Strategic Management.* New York: John Wiley & Sons, 1983.

Henderson, Carter. *Winners.* New York: Holt, Rinehart & Winston, 1985.

Hickman, Craig R. *The Strategy Game.* New York: McGraw-Hill, 1993.

King, William R., and David I. Cleland. *Strategic Planning and Management Handbook.* New York: Van Nostrand Reinhold, 1987.

Jones, Patricia, and Larry Kahaner. *Say It and Live It.* New York: Currency-Doubleday, 1995.

Kotler, Philip, William Fahey, and S. Jatusripitak. *The New Competition.* Englewood Cliffs, NJ: Prentice-Hall, 1985.

Krause, Donald G. *The Art of War for Executives.* New York: Perigee Books, 1995.

Lele, Milind M. *Creating Strategic Leverage.* New York: John Wiley & Sons, 1992.

Mintzberg, Henry. *The Rise and Fall of Strategic Planning.* New York: Free Press, 1994.

Mintzberg, Henry, Bruce Ahlstrand, and Joseph Lampel. *Strategy Safari.* New York: Free Press, 1998.

Mintzberg, Henry, and James Brian Quinn. *The Strategy Process.* Englewood Cliffs, NJ: Prentice-Hall, 1992.

Moore, J. I. *Writers on Strategy and Strategic Management.* New York: Penguin Books, 1992.

Morris, David J., Jr. *Market Power and Business Strategy.* Westport, CT: Quorum Books, 1996.

Morita, Akio. *Made in Japan.* New York: E. P. Dutton, 1986.

Pattison, Joseph E. *Breaking Boundaries.* Princeton, NJ: Patersons/Pacesettter Books, 1996.

Perry, Lee Tom, Randall G. Scott, and W. Norman Smallwood. *Real-Time Strategy.* New York: John Wiley & Sons, 1993.

Porter, Michael. *Competitive Advantage.* New York: Free Press, 1985.

Porter, Michael. *Competitive Strategy.* New York: Free Press, 1980.

Quigley, Joseph V. *Vision.* New York: McGraw-Hill, 1993.

Rich, Stanley R., and David Gumpert. *Business Plans That Win Dollars.* New York: Harper & Row, 1985.

Robert, Michel. *Strategic Thinking.* Westport, CT: Decision Processes, 1981.

Robert, Michel. *Strategy Pure and Simple.* New York: McGraw-Hill, 1993.

Robert, Michel. *Strategy Pure and Simple II.* New York: McGraw-Hill, 1997.

Robert, Michel. *The Strategist CEO.* Westport, CT: Quorum Books, 1988.

Rothchild, William E. *How to Gain and Maintain the Competitive Edge in Business.* New York: McGraw-Hill, 1984.

Rothchild, William E. *Putting It All Together.* New York: AMACOM, 1986

Rumelt, Richard P., Dan E. Schendel, and David J. Teece. *Fundamental Issues in Strategy.* Boston, MA: Harvard Business School Press, 1994.

Sawyer, Ralph D. *Sun Tzu: The Art of War.* Boulder, CO: Westview Press, 1994.

Schaffer, Robert H. *The Breakthrough Strategy.* Cambridge, MA: Harper & Row, 1988.

Shanklin, William L., and John K. Ryans, Jr. *Thinking Strategically.* New York: Random House, 1985.

Shenkman, Michael H. *The Strategic Heart.* Westport, CT: Quorum Books, 1996.

Sirower, Mark L. *The Synergy Trap.* New York: Free Press, 1997.

Sloan, Alfred P. *My Years with General Motors.* New York: Doubleday, 1972.

Steiner, George A. *Strategic Planning.* New York: Free Press, 1979.

Von Senger, Harro. *The Book of Stratagems.* New York: Viking Press, 1991.

Waddell, William C. *The Outline of Strategy.* Oxford, OH: Planning Forum, 1986.

Wing, R. L. *The Art of Strategy.* New York: Doubleday, 1988.

Yip, George S. *Total Global Strategy.* Englewood Cliffs, NJ: Prentice-Hall, 1992.

Index

About the Author

Michel Robert is founder and president of Decision Processes International, Inc., an internationally known consulting firm with 40 partners in 15 countries. His clients include such major companies as Caterpillar, 3M, and GATX. A noted speaker, he has written articles in numerous business magazines and journals, including *Forbes, Barron's, Harvard Business Review, Fortune, The Wall Street Journal, Time,* and *Business Week.* He is the author of *Strategy Pure & Simple, Product Innovation Strategy Pure & Simple,* and *Strategy Pure & Simple II.* Robert lives in Westport, CT.